chow down
& chill out

chow down
& chill out

fast asian recipes for busy people

Jennifer Yee

RANDOM HOUSE
NEW ZEALAND

For my family and the special friends I eat and laugh with, who have also shared their kitchens, food and cooking wisdom with me.

Thanks to Oriental Merchant for their generous support in this project and for quality Asian pantry ingredients to work with.

Acknowledgements: Grateful thanks to Eon Design Centre, Collinson private collection, Corso De Fiori, Living & Giving, Simon Gault tableware from Gault@George, Stevens Home & Giving — St Lukes and Zenophile Ltd for kindly supplying table and homeware. Superb Herb Company for super herbs.

And to the team, huge thanks — Alan and Anna for your brilliant photographic skills, friendship and guidance; Rosie and Sarah-Jane for help with food preparation and props; David, Jo, Mandy and Neil for all you do.

National Library of New Zealand Cataloguing-in-Publication Data

Yee, Jennifer, BHSc.
Chow down & chill out : fast Asian recipes for busy people / Jennifer Yee.
Includes index.
ISBN 1-86941-589-2
1. Cookery, Asian. 2. Quick and easy cookery. I. Title.
641.595—dc 21

A RANDOM HOUSE BOOK
published by
Random House New Zealand
18 Poland Road, Glenfield, Auckland, New Zealand
www.randomhouse.co.nz

First published 2003

ISBN 1 86941 589 2

Design and layout: Nick Turzynski
Colour photography: Alan Gillard
Black and white photography: Anna Comrie-Thomson
Picture on p.47 Daniel Hung

Printed in Hong Kong

contents

introduction

CHOW DOWN AND CHILL OUT — that's all I really want to do at the end of a busy day. With just a few simple basics in the larder you can be ready to throw together some tasty, aromatic dishes with Asian ingredients as your inspiration. Add to these core recipes a tangle of noodles, a bowl of steaming rice or ready-to-go dumplings and you can have a stunning meal ready in half an hour — meals that you flash in the wok and serve up straight from the pan, hot, fast and furiously stir-fried. Most of the recipes in this book fall into this framework although I do explore a range of techniques, and make use of the oven and barbecue.

At other times all you may feel up to is an easy one-bowl meal that you can eat curled up in front of the telly — no table to set and less washing up puts a smile on anyone's face! Taking time to chill out is as important as preparing something nourishingly good but simple.

eating asian style

Asian meals at home are a pretty relaxed affair once you're all gathered around the table. The flurry of activity behind the scenes can seem frenetic to the timid, but life revolves around meals for nearly all Asians and most of the family are keen to muck in, save the odd teenager.

There will almost always be a tureen of soup, a meat dish, a seafood or fish dish and a salad or a plate of greens, whether you're eating Vietnamese or Malay. Possibly a vegetarian dish of silken tofu or fat, fragrant shiitake mushrooms will be added. There'll be a range of condiments so that you can add more chilli, more savoury, more tang or the fragrance of shallot oil. Whatever you add, the balance of texture, flavour and aroma should elicit joy. There is a Cantonese compliment — to say that your food is 'song hou' means that it is 'pleasure in the mouth'.

getting started

With a little smart planning you can soon equip your kitchen with the ingredients needed to handle a range of delicious Asian dishes at short notice. By having the following essentials at your fingertips, you can transform the ordinary into something special without too many headaches. You will also appear highly organised — a good thing for any great cook.

Use the following shopping lists as guides to build up an army of ingredients to have at the ready. Many of the pantry basics are now available in the Asian food section of your local supermarket and all can be found in Asian food stores. For fresh items, look in the produce section or spend a weekend morning exploring your local growers' market.

If you need extra help, my book *Discovering Asian Ingredients* explains it all in more detail, along with pictures to help you identify items, including Asian greens and herbs.

STARTER ASIAN PANTRY
Basic starter pack of 10 items

- light and dark soy sauces
- fish sauce
- oyster sauce
- chilli sauce (choose between sweet chilli, chilli bean, sambal oelek or any other favourite)
- sesame oil
- jasmine rice
- rice vermicelli or rice stick noodles
- dried egg noodles
- Thai curry paste or laksa paste
- Szechwan peppercorns

With these basic sauces, dried goods and meal helpers you can cook a wide range of Asian dishes. Over time, or as a recipe calls for them, add rice paper wrappers, udon, soba and somen noodles, bean thread vermicelli and some flavour accents such as palm sugar, wasabi paste, Japanese rice wine vinegar, rice wine, star anise, sweet soy sauce and tamarind. As a flavouring, tamarind can come from fresh tamarind, tamarind pulp, paste or water. By including these you will soon build a pantry that will enable you to tackle a number of Asian cuisines easily.

Choose quality brands of spice pastes, for example Valcom, for when you don't have the urge to pound or whiz up your own fresh spice pastes. But do try to make one from scratch at least once a year, when all the wet spices are in season, for a true lift for your senses. When using spice paste, I often add fresh herbs to liven them up and add zing.

Five 'must haves' for the freezer

- chicken, fish or beef stock (1-litre lots, frozen in plastic bags)
- coconut milk, frozen in ice cube trays
- wonton or gow gee wrappers
- 'hard' herbs such as lemon grass and kaffir lime leaves
- chillies (a mixture of hot and mild)

With these meal starters in your freezer, you will be able to pull together a soup, a heady curry, some dumplings, and add another dimension of flavour to your cooking. Braising liquids, cooled and frozen in flat plastic bags, are also handy so don't discard them. Bones for stock can be accumulated for the basis of a good soup — they will take up a bit of freezer space though.

Weekly buys

- wet spices such as ginger, garlic, shallots
- fresh herbs such as coriander, chives, lemon grass, kaffir lime leaves
- Thai sweet basil, laksa leaf or Vietnamese mint, when in season

I'm fortunate to be able to obtain fresh herbs such as lemon grass and kaffir lime leaves year-round from a Thai woman at the weekend markets. She and her husband grow superb quality produce to supply Thai restaurants around the country. When chillies are in season, I tend to buy a mixture of red, green, purple/black and orange chillies ranging from 'dynamite' chillies to the milder long red chillies and freeze them to use when required.

If you don't find these fresh products readily accessible, check out the authentic Asian section of your supermarket for quality bottled lemon grass, kaffir lime leaves and chillies. They are a good stand-by when fresh produce is not in season or hard to find. Once opened, store them in the fridge.

Staples to fill up on

A tangle of noodles, a bowl of steaming rice or ready-to-go dumplings, flat breads or buns. These are basics that are easy to prepare, readily available and ensure you don't go hungry — they are the 'potatoes' of the Asian table.

Use your noodle

With a selection of different types of noodles at the ready you will always be able to provide a meal in less than half an hour. Learn to master cooking these — most of them need only brief cooking in boiling water or soaking and softening in hot water then draining before use. Rinse noodles under cold water to stop them from overcooking and to help them retain that 'al dente' bite. Prepared this way they are ready to be wokked, tossed with salad ingredients, herbs, dressings or dipped into condiments (as for soba noodles) or used to form the base of a fast meal-in-a-bowl soup.

Generally noodle dishes can be classified into wet (soupy, with a gravy) or dry (with little or no sauce). Both types lend themselves to adding chilli in all its forms. For a bit of kick, you can add fresh chopped chillies and quartered limes, chilli oil, chilli jam or sweet chilli sauce, sambal, chilli bean sauce or crushed dried chillies.

smart little helpers

Some foods don't need much embellishment, but the right garnish or accompaniment can transform even the simplest food into something that looks and tastes special. Take fresh oysters — perfection on their own but with mirin, grated daikon radish, spring onion, and a drizzle of peanut oil you get transported to your own Japanese eatery.

I always keep some light soy sauce and wasabi handy for when we go fishing — we can have instant sashimi. Otherwise fresh fish fillets, quickly pan-fried on a portable barbecue or in a frying pan over a small camp stove, can be dipped into ready made Salt and Szechwan Pepper Mix with a squeeze of fresh limes for Vietnamese-style fish!

Here are some great stand-bys that will make life that much easier:

asian noodle dressing

4 tablespoons fish sauce
2 tablespoons sweet chilli sauce
2 teaspoons sesame oil
juice of 2 small limes
2 fresh kaffir lime leaves, midrib removed and shredded
2 tablespoons palm sugar, shaved with a sharp knife
4 tablespoons mint leaves
¼ cup coriander leaves
¼ cup Thai sweet basil leaves

Mix together the sauces, oil, lime juice and kaffir lime leaves. Add the palm sugar and stir to dissolve. Adjust the flavours to taste if necessary. Toss the dressing and the herbs through any noodle-based salad and enjoy!

MAKES ABOUT 1 CUP

spring onion and ginger dip

2 spring onions, very finely chopped
1 tablespoon grated ginger
½ teaspoon salt
2 tablespoons water
2 teaspoons sesame oil

Pound together the spring onions and ginger using a mortar and pestle until a paste is formed and then stir in the other ingredients. This dip is also delicious with roasted meats.

MAKES ABOUT ½ CUP

asian drizzle

2 tablespoons mirin
1 teaspoon chilli black bean
  sauce
1 teaspoon sesame oil
zest and juice of 1–2
  fresh limes
1 tablespoon light
  soy sauce
1 tablespoon fish sauce
1 tablespoon grated ginger
½ teaspoon Salt and Szechwan
  Pepper Mix (see opposite)

Blend all the ingredients together and serve in a small bowl with a teaspoon for drizzling over fresh oysters and steamed or pan-fried fish. Try it tossed through quickly stir-fried vegetables, or chunks of hot, roasted pumpkin and kumara or other root vegetables. A great treat for a crowd is fresh Pacific oysters in the half shell with wedges of lime and the sauce in a bowl to drizzle over. Before serving them on a bed of crushed ice, loosen the oysters with a sharp knife. This allows for fast and easy slipping straight into mouths! Provide plenty of napkins.

asian drizzle (left) and
ginger shallot and
chilli sauce (right)

ginger, shallot and chilli sauce

About 5 years ago I tried a similar store-bought product made by a reputable Asian supplier, but I figured that it would be even better made using fresh ingredients and this has since become a regular hero in my 'chilled pantry' (refrigerator). It's a flavoursome little helper I can't do without. Here is a good quantity to make and to have on stand-by for those meals where you just can't be bothered with more than 4–5 ingredients. Use it in marinades, as a dipping sauce for roasted and steeped Asian-style chicken, in egg foo young-type omelettes and to toss through stir-fries.

½ cup salad oil
1 teaspoon sesame oil
¾ cup finely chopped ginger
½ cup finely chopped shallots
3–4 red chillies (the small
  bird's eye chillies), seeded
  and sliced
2 teaspoons salt

Heat the oils in a small saucepan until hot. Add the ginger, shallots, chilli and salt, reduce the heat and cook until the shallots are translucent. Do not brown. Remove from the heat and allow to cool before packing into a clean plastic tub or jar. This will keep sealed and refrigerated for up to 3 months. Use a clean spoon each time it is used.

MAKES 1 CUP

Variation: Leave out the chilli if you are a wimp.

coriander and cashew pesto

This is superb dolloped onto grilled, baked or barbecued seafood or meats, particularly tender lamb cutlets. Try it on roasted vegetables or barbecued asparagus. You can also give it a chilli kick by adding a green or red chilli.

2 well-packed cups fresh
    coriander leaves
2 cloves garlic, peeled
3 tablespoons chopped ginger
1 kaffir lime leaf, finely
    shredded
1 cup dry-roasted cashews
½ teaspoon sesame oil
2 tablespoons toasted
    sesame seeds
2 tablespoons light soy sauce
1 teaspoon mirin
1 tablespoon fish sauce
½ cup sunflower, corn or light
    olive oil
extra oil

Put all the ingredients except the sunflower oil into a food processor bowl and blend until everything is finely chopped. Drizzle the oil in through the feed tube with the motor running, and process until thick and smooth. Spoon into clean, sterilised jars and cover the surface of the pesto with a little extra oil. This will keep in the refrigerator for at least a week.

MAKES ABOUT 2½ CUPS

salt and szechwan pepper mix (left) and coriander and cashew pesto (right)

salt and szechwan pepper mix

This flavoured salt is used traditionally as a dip for Cantonese crispy skin chicken or for Salt, Pepper and Chilli Prawns (see page 56).

Toast ¼ to ½ cup Szechwan peppercorns until fragrant in a dry frying pan. Cool and grind until fine, using a mortar and pestle or spice grinder. Pass through a coarse sieve if necessary to remove any large pieces of husk from the pepper berries. Mix with an equal quantity of sea salt or salt flakes. Store in an airtight jar or serve at the table in small 'pinch pots' for individuals to season their own food.

eating with family and friends

The best thing about sharing an Asian meal is that you do just that. There is a conviviality about sitting around the table and sharing dishes of food. Most Asian meals are not individual offerings arranged on a plate with portions that need attacking with knife and fork. Food is mostly cut into mouth-sized pieces to be eaten with chopsticks or from a spoon or both.

GREEN BEANS WITH PORK AND CHINESE OLIVES

ASIAN LAMB AND VEGETABLE STIR-FRY

CHI AI'S LEMON GRASS GINGER CHICKEN

KAFFIR LIME AND RED CURRY DIP FOR FISH

TEMPURA BEER BATTER

HAWKER-STYLE FRIED RICE NOODLES

ASIAN GREENS FOR A CROWD

    START WITH CHOY SUM

GAI LAN (BROCCOLI GREENS) WITH BLACK BEAN BEEF

MUSHROOMS WITH SPICY BLACK BEAN BEEF

HANOI TURMERIC SALMON WITH DILL

    FISH SAUCE DRESSING

    SHRIMP AND ORANGE SAUCE

ROAST BELLY PORK

It's okay to slurp and make enthusiastic noises and the more clatter, laughter and general raucousness the better.

green beans with pork and chinese olives

May and Ching run the Canton Cafe, Auckland's best home-style Cantonese restaurant. It's packed out every night by Chinese, locals and professional chefs. There's been a queue at the door most nights since it opened. Here's my version of a favourite dish I like to eat there.

250g shoulder pork
1 tablespoon Shao Hsing rice wine
¼ teaspoon salt
½ teaspoon sugar
2 tablespoons light soy sauce
1 tablespoon oyster sauce
500g green beans
1 tablespoon corn, peanut or light olive oil
2 cloves garlic, chopped
3 tablespoons chopped Chinese dried, salted olives
1 teaspoon sugar
2 tablespoons cold water

Chop the pork into a coarse mince or cut across the grain into fine strips. Mix in a bowl with the rice wine, salt, sugar, soy and oyster sauce. Leave to marinate for 10 minutes.

String and trim beans if necessary, and cut or snap in half.

Heat the oil in a wok until hot and add the garlic, olives, sugar and the marinated pork. Stir-fry for 2 minutes or until the pork is lightly browned and cooked through. Remove to a warm dish and immediately add the beans and the water to lift the juices off the base of the wok and to create steam. Toss the beans to ensure they cook evenly. When tender, add the meat back into the wok and mix together. Serve hot with rice and 1–2 other dishes.

SERVES 4 AS A SIDE DISH

asian lamb and vegetable stir-fry

Marinade

1 clove garlic, crushed

1 tablespoon finely chopped
 ginger

3 tablespoons black pepper
 sauce

1 tablespoon hoisin sauce

2 tablespoons oyster sauce

1 tablespoon light soy sauce

350g lean lamb leg steaks or
 schnitzel

2 tablespoons vegetable oil

1 red onion, sliced

1 cup broccoli flowerets

3 courgettes, sliced diagonally

1 cup sliced green beans

1–2 tablespoons water

½ teaspoon salt

½ teaspoon sugar

1 tablespoon Shao Hsing rice
 wine or dry sherry

1 tablespoon water, extra

1 teaspoon cornflour

Mix the marinade ingredients together in a bowl. Slice the lamb into strips, place in the marinade and leave to marinate for 10–15 minutes.

Heat a frying pan or wok until hot, drizzle in 1 tablespoon of the oil and swirl to coat the pan. Add the onion and fry until softened, then add the lamb and stir-fry for about 4 minutes or until lightly browned or cooked to your liking. Remove from the wok to a dish and keep warm.

Rinse and dry the wok if you wish, although this is not necessary. Add the remaining tablespoon of oil to the pan and heat until hot before adding the broccoli. Toss until the flowerets start turning a bright green colour then add the courgettes and beans. Stir-fry for 1–2 minutes, then sprinkle with the water to create steam and place a lid briefly over the vegetables (about 1 minute) to cook them through. Season with salt and sugar and mix through. Add the cooked lamb to the wok and stir-fry for a minute, then stir in the rice wine mixed with the extra water and cornflour. Bring to the boil to thicken (it should form a light glaze), then spoon onto a warm plate.

SERVES 3–4 WITH OTHER DISHES AND RICE

chi ai's lemon grass ginger chicken

Vietnam has become my adopted home. It may be the fragrance of herbs and the slipperiness of the noodles that does it, or possibly the freedom to drift from being Asian to being a foreign visitor. I've been fortunate to have experienced family kitchens so basic that wood or coal is still used, and have also had the privilege of being able to work alongside chefs in 5-star establishments with international reputations. Chi Ai (Aunty Ai) runs a family restaurant in Hue, Vietnam, serving home-style meals. Her lemon grass chicken is punched with flavour and few of the big city restaurants even come close to this recipe.

500g (about 4) chicken thigh fillets
1 teaspoon salt
a few grinds black pepper
2 cloves garlic, minced
2 tablespoons finely chopped ginger
10cm piece lemon grass, thinly sliced
1 red chilli, sliced
½ red onion, chopped
2 tablespoons sunflower or other light vegetable oil
3 tablespoons shaved palm sugar
3 tablespoons fish sauce
¼ cup water
2 spring onions, chopped

Slice each chicken thigh fillet in half lengthwise, trim away excess fat and then slice across the grain into thin strips. Place in a bowl with the salt, pepper, garlic, ginger, lemon grass, chilli and onion. Allow to marinate for 15 minutes. (You can get the rice on to cook and prepare any vegetables in this time.)

Heat the oil in a wok or heavy frying pan until hot. Add the chicken and stir-fry for 2 minutes until golden. Lower the heat and sprinkle the palm sugar over, allowing it to caramelise in the pan juices for about 1 minute. Blend the fish sauce with the water and add it to the wok. Cover with a lid and simmer gently for 5 minutes, allowing the flavours to marry together. Turn off the heat and toss the spring onions through.

Tip into a warmed dish for serving. Spoon over bowls of hot jasmine rice. Accompanied with a vegetable dish such as mustard greens cooked in a little chicken stock, this makes a quick, flavour-punched meal.

SERVES 3–4

kaffir lime and red curry dip for fish

An addictive Thai chilli dip for serving with mouthfuls of tempura-battered fish and steamed green beans or other vegetables. Try it also as a spread on toasted flat breads such as naan or pide.

1 cup red curry paste
3–4 cloves garlic
1–2 shallots, sliced
lemon grass
vegetable oil
1 tablespoon fish sauce
1 tablespoon lime juice
1 tablespoon shaved palm
** sugar**
2 kaffir lime leaves
coconut cream

The red curry paste is pounded with the garlic, shallots and 10cm of the bulb end of lemon grass, thinly sliced. This is fried in the smallest amount of oil to toast and bring out the flavours, before being blended with the fish sauce, lime juice and shaved palm sugar. Two finely shredded kaffir lime leaves are stirred through before spooning into dishes for dipping. It is then dressed with a drizzle of coconut cream to finish.

MAKES 1½ CUPS

tempura beer batter

This is as close to my dad's excellent batter as it gets — he never measures, but intuitively gets it right each time. His battered fish is the fish of champions, as are his tempura-style Bluff oysters and green shell mussels. Make sure the beer is truly icy cold for the lightest results.

⅓ cup cornflour
⅔ cup plain flour
¼ teaspoon salt
a few grinds black pepper
1–1½ cups ice cold lager or
** pilsener-style beer**
¼ cup chopped coriander
** (optional)**

Sift the flours and seasonings into a bowl. Whisk in the beer, blending until smooth. The batter should be the thickness of pouring cream, so add sufficient cold beer to obtain the right consistency. Add the coriander if using. Use the batter when it is still slightly foamy from the addition of the beer.

This batter is ideal for thinly sliced vegetables such as pumpkin, choko, sugar snap peas or small, fresh whole fish or fish fillets cut into thick fingers. Lightly coat your choice of vegetables or fish in some seasoned flour, shaking to remove any excess. Dip 1 piece into the batter at a time, then lower into hot oil and fry until crispy. Drain on paper towels and serve hot.

MAKES ABOUT 2½ CUPS

hawker-style fried rice noodles

This Malay dish, char kueh teow, of spicy fresh rice noodles with prawns, squid and Chinese sausage is addictive! It is a popular recipe on hawker stalls and typifies Asian street food — served at a pace that is fast, loud and furious. You can have some fun by serving these noodles to your guests in American-style Chinese takeaway pottles along with disposable wooden chopsticks.

1kg fresh rice noodles or 500g dried rice stick noodles
vegetable oil or peanut oil
2 cloves garlic, crushed
1 fresh red chilli, sliced, or ½–1 tablespoon chilli bean sauce
200g uncooked prawn meat or green prawns, shelled and deveined
200g baby squid tubes, sliced into strips, or criss-crossed pieces (see below)
3 cooked Chinese sausages, sliced diagonally
2 tablespoons light soy sauce
1 tablespoon dark soy sauce
1 tablespoon oyster sauce
1 large handful fresh mung bean sprouts
1 spring onion, sliced
½ cup roughly chopped fresh coriander

If you are using fresh rice noodles straight from the refrigerator prepare them by placing in a colander and pouring boiling water over them. If the fresh noodles are soft and pliable, separate them and set aside.

Heat sufficient oil to coat a large non-stick frying pan or wok. When the oil is hot, add the garlic and chilli (or chilli bean sauce) and toss until fragrant. Tip in the prawns, squid and sausages. Stir-fry for 2–3 minutes or until the prawns have lost their translucency and the squid has curled up. Add the sauces, then the noodles and bean sprouts, tossing to combine all ingredients. Cook for a further 2–3 minutes over a high heat, until the noodles are hot. Scatter with the spring onion and coriander and serve either in warmed noodle bowls or piled onto plates. Eat straight away!

SERVES 4–5

To make squid scrolls
Cut the squid tubes along one side so they open out flat, forming a rectangular sheet. Score the surface without cutting right through the squid, making diagonal cuts across the sheet. Turn the squid 90 degrees and repeat, making a criss-cross pattern. Cut the sheet into two pieces.

asian greens for a crowd

The worst thing you can do when cooking Asian greens is to cook them without moisture. They need a quick blanch and a slick of oil before charring, or a splash of rice wine or water before wokking. The important thing to remember is that bok choy, gai lan, choy sum and their cousins like to have their leaves hot, wet and steamy. Think 'sauna' and you'll get it right.

Blanching method

Wash and trim the ends from a bunch of choy sum. Pour boiling water from the kettle into a large pan and season with salt to taste. Add 1 tablespoon of vegetable oil and bring to the boil. Drop the choy sum into the boiling water and turn the vegetables to ensure even cooking. Wait until the water comes to the boil again and turn off the heat. The stems should be tender but still crisp, and lightly coated and glossy from the oil. Drain and transfer to a warmed serving dish. If you wish, you can cut the stems into shorter lengths to make them more manageable, or serve them restaurant style — left whole and arranged so that all the stem ends are bunched together. Try drizzling with oyster sauce and eating with rice, noodles and other dishes.

Moist fry/steam method

Wash and trim the ends from the choy sum, then cut the stems and leaves into even-sized pieces about 10cm long. Heat the oil in a wok or large frying pan and add the stems first. Toss until these start to change to a bright green colour, then add the leaves. Toss again and sprinkle with 1–2 tablespoons of cold water. Place a lid over the wok or pan briefly to create steam, which will cook the greens and also keep them moist. When you hear a crackling sound, lift the lid and toss the vegetables quickly. Test the stems to see if they are tender or need further cooking. When cooked, serve immediately.

start with choy sum

These recipes are easily multiplied to serve a crowd by increasing the number of bunches of greens and flavourings. One bunch of choy sum serves 3–4 as a side dish.

1 bunch choy sum
  (Chinese flowering cabbage)

choy sum with garlic oil

Cook the greens using one of the methods on page 23. Heat 2 tablespoons vegetable oil in a small saucepan with 1–2 cloves crushed garlic until fragrant and sizzling. Pour carefully over the cooked greens.

choy sum with toasted sesame seeds and sesame oil

Toast 1 tablespoon of sesame seeds in a dry, non-stick pan until golden. You will need to keep the seeds moving by swirling the pan while you brown them to ensure an even colour. Toss about ½ teaspoon of sesame oil through the drained and cooked choy sum and serve sprinkled with the toasted seeds.

choy sum on crispy noodles with pork stir-fry

Preheat the oven to 200°C. Prepare fine egg noodles by pouring boiling water over them until softened, or cook according to the packet directions. Drain well and toss with about 1 teaspoon each of vegetable and sesame oil for 2 nests or skeins of noodles. Season with freshly ground or crushed Szechwan pepper and about 1 tablespoon of oyster sauce. Spread the noodles onto an ovenproof dish and place in the hot oven. When golden brown, turn with tongs to crisp the other side. Watch the noodles carefully to stop them from burning. Lift onto a warm serving dish. Top with cooked choy sum and a simple stir-fry of pork strips marinated with soy sauce, salt, sugar, pepper, Shao Hsing wine and shredded ginger.

choy sum with garlic oil

gai lan (broccoli greens) with black bean beef

Gai lan or Chinese broccoli greens have the appearance of velvety grey/green broccoli leaves. The stems should be no thicker than your index finger, but if you can easily pierce the stem with your fingernail they will be tender. Peel or trim off any stems that may be fibrous. Both the leaves and stems are edible and can be blanched or stir-fried. A good substitute is broccolini.

Marinade

½ teaspoon salt
pinch of freshly ground Szechwan peppercorns
1 tablespoon light soy sauce
1 teaspoon sugar

Beef

150g rump steak, cut into thin slices across the grain
1 tablespoon vegetable or peanut oil
3 slices ginger, finely julienned
1 clove garlic, finely chopped
1½ tablespoons salted black beans, soaked in warm water for 5 minutes then drained
1 red chilli, seeded and finely chopped (optional)
1 tablespoon Shao Hsing rice wine or dry sherry
1 tablespoon water
1 teaspoon cornflour

Greens

500g gai lan
1 tablespoon vegetable or peanut oil
1–2 tablespoons water
½ teaspoon salt
¼ teaspoon sugar

Mix the marinade ingredients together, combine with the meat slices and leave to marinate for 10 minutes.

Next prepare the greens. Trim the stems and peel any fibrous stalks. Cut the stems into 2 or 3 portions. Heat a frying pan or wok until hot, drizzle the oil in and swirl to coat the pan. Add the gai lan stems and toss several times to lightly coat with the oil. When the stems are just changing colour, add the leaves to the wok and stir-fry until bright green. Sprinkle with the water to create steam and place a lid briefly over the vegetables (about 1–2 minutes) to cook them through. Season with salt and sugar and toss. Remove from the wok and keep warm.

Rinse and dry the wok, then heat it. Add the oil for the beef, the ginger, garlic, black beans and chilli if using. Stir into the oil and then add the marinated beef and stir-fry for about 4 minutes before adding the gai lan to the pan. Stir all together for a minute and then pour in the rice wine mixed with the water and cornflour, stir through the meat and greens. Bring to the boil to thicken (it should form a light glaze); spoon onto a warm plate.

SERVES 3–4 WITH OTHER DISHES AND RICE

mushrooms with spicy black bean beef

Instead of the flat portobello mushrooms you can use any of the fresh Asian mushrooms now available. Substitute with shiitake for a more woodsy flavour or try a mixture of enokitake (golden needle), wood ear and oyster mushrooms, but cook them only briefly as they are much more delicate.

250g portobello mushrooms or a mixture of Asian mushrooms
200g beef schnitzel
1 tablespoon finely chopped ginger
1 tablespoon light soy sauce
1 tablespoon black bean and garlic sauce
1 red chilli, finely chopped (optional)
½ teaspoon sugar
few grinds black pepper or ¼ teaspoon Szechwan pepper
½ teaspoon cornflour
vegetable oil
1 tablespoon coarsely chopped coriander

Slice the mushrooms into thick strips and set aside. Next, slice the beef into thin strips. Place in a medium-sized bowl and add the ginger, sauces, chilli, seasonings and cornflour. Mix well and marinate for 10–15 minutes if time allows.

Pour enough oil into a clean frying pan to coat the base and heat until hot. Add the marinated beef and stir-fry quickly until lightly browned. Do not over-cook. Transfer the beef to a dish and keep warm.

Heat 1–2 tablespoons of oil in the frying pan until hot. Add the mushrooms and stir-fry until lightly browned and tender. Turn off the heat and return the beef to the pan with the coriander, tossing to mix with the mushrooms.

Spoon into a serving dish and serve hot with rice and a plate of vegetables such as choy sum or gai lan.

SERVES 3–4

hanoi turmeric salmon with dill

This has been an often-requested dish; in fact, my friend Neil has been known to call me especially when he has withdrawal symptoms! It's also a hot favourite at my cooking classes. A golden, shimmering turmeric fish recipe, this adaptation is from a hundred-year-old recipe from the Cha Ca La Vong restaurant in the Hanoi Old Quarter, Vietnam. Cha Ca simply means fried fish. This is the only dish that is served at the restaurant and the original recipe uses twice-fried catfish, which you cook over a glowing clay brazier at your table. Tuna or snapper also work well in this recipe but the rich, moist flesh of fresh salmon is the ultimate with rice noodles or a steaming bowl of rice!

500g piece of salmon fillet, cut into thick strips, pin-bones removed
2 teaspoons sunflower oil
½ teaspoon freshly ground Szechwan peppercorns
½ teaspoon salt
2 tablespoons grated fresh turmeric
4 spring onions
1 cup roughly chopped dill
extra oil for cooking

Mix the fish, oil, seasonings and turmeric together in a bowl. Trim off the green spring onion tops and cut these into 4cm lengths. Slice the white part thinly into strips. Set aside with the dill.

Heat enough oil to coat the base of a frying pan or wok until just starting to smoke. Tip in the salmon and toss gently to seal the outside of the fish. Add all of the herbs and mix through. Try to do this without breaking up the fish. The herbs will wilt from the heat of the pan and the salmon should be just cooked. Remove the pan from the element immediately and spoon the fish into a heated serving dish.

For serving:
3–4 servings ribbon-cut fresh rice sheet noodles or cooked rice vermicelli
small bunch Thai sweet basil
freshly roasted peanuts, coarsely chopped
Fish Sauce Dressing (see page 30)
Shrimp and Orange Sauce (see page 30)

Have ready plates of rice noodles or rice vermicelli for everyone to help themselves from and provide each person with a rice bowl and chopsticks. Serve the dressings, peanuts and sprigs of basil in separate bowls to pass around. Each person places some noodles into their bowl, tops this with several spoonfuls of fish, some peanuts, some basil and then their choice of the dressings.

Serves 3–4 as a light first course or 2–3 hungry eaters as a main dish.

This recipe can be doubled easily.

fish sauce dressing

This flavour-packed fish sauce dressing is served at nearly every Vietnamese meal and is used to accompany many delicious grilled meat and rice noodle dishes along with a table salad of lettuce and fresh herbs.

1–2 small red chillies, finely chopped
1 tablespoon white vinegar or wine vinegar
½ cup fish sauce
¼ cup fresh lime juice
1 small carrot, finely julienned, rinsed and pressed dry between paper towels (optional)
2 cloves garlic, minced
½ cup sugar or grated palm sugar
1½ cups warm water

Blend all the ingredients together in a bowl, stirring until the sugar has dissolved. Taste the dressing and adjust the flavourings if necessary. Serve at room temperature. Stored in a jar, this dressing will keep refrigerated for up to 5 days.

If the water is omitted the sauce will keep for months in the fridge. Dilute before using with 1 part dressing to 1 part water, or to taste.

MAKES ABOUT 2 ½ CUPS

shrimp and orange sauce

This is a robust-flavoured sauce so you won't need much! The orange zest and juice mellow out the sauce on standing — trust me, it's addictive.

1 small clove garlic
¼ teaspoon grated orange zest
1 teaspoon Lee Kum Kee fine shrimp sauce
½ teaspoon chilli oil
3 tablespoons fresh orange juice

Blend the garlic, orange zest and shrimp sauce in a mortar and pestle until smooth. Mix in the chilli oil and orange juice. Tip into a small bowl and stand for 20 minutes before serving to allow the flavours to infuse. Cover any leftover sauce before storing in the refrigerator. It will keep for up to 5 days.

MAKES ABOUT ¼ CUP

roast belly pork

Few of us have had the opportunity of seeing a whole pig being roasted in a specially built oven until the skin is almost the colour of red lacquer. To achieve this distinctive crackling, some old advice is never to score the skin and never to use pork that has been frozen, as the skin will not crisp up. Drying the skin gives a better crackling, and one method was to hang the pork in a windy place overnight until the skin was very dry. However, a similar effect can be achieved at home using a piece of pork from the middle section of the belly, with the skin or rind left on. I've used my grandmother's method to eliminate the air-drying. She was a smart cook.

1.5kg belly pork in 1 piece, without spareribs
boiling water
½ teaspoon salt

Marinade

1 teaspoon salt
1 teaspoon sugar
1 tablespoon ground brown bean sauce
1 tablespoon hoisin sauce
½ teaspoon light soy sauce
1 teaspoon five-spice powder

Dips

dark soy sauce
hoisin sauce
plum sauce

Preheat the oven to 200°C. Place a roasting rack in the sink and lay the pork belly on top, skin side facing up. Pour boiling water over the skin. It will shrink slightly. Wipe the pork skin dry with a paper towel. Using a fork with close-set, sharp tines, or the tip of a sharp knife, pierce the skin rind vigorously and repeatedly until it is entirely covered with fine holes. Rub the salt all over the skin. Make horizontal cuts on the flesh side, about 2.5cm apart and 1cm deep.

Prepare the marinade by mixing all the ingredients together in a small bowl. Using the back of a spoon, spread the marinade onto the flesh side and into the grooves. Do not smear any marinade along the sides of the pork, otherwise they will be burned when roasted.

Place the pork, skin side up, on a rack in the top half of the oven over a tray of hot water to catch the drippings. Roast for 15 minutes at 200°C and then reduce the oven temperature to 190°C for about 1 hour. Do not open the oven door at all until it is time to test whether the pork is done. Test by piercing the meat with a skewer or chopstick; if it goes in easily and the juices that run out are clear and not pink, the pork is done. The skin will have turned into excellent crackling.

Rest the pork on a board for a few minutes. Carve into 1–2.5cm slices with a cleaver or a sharp, serrated meat carver. Transfer to a warm serving dish and serve with the dips.

SERVES 4

Note: You can purchase ground brown bean sauce, or else use brown bean sauce and mash with the back of a spoon.

for two

There is nothing nicer than to just chill out with a mate and share a dish or two with a great bottle of delicious wine. Whether that person is your best friend, a parent, sibling or your soul mate, they will probably be someone who also cooks for you. These recipes are for those special times.

SOUL SOUP WITH COCKLES AND KICK

SPICY BASIL CHICKEN

HOPPING GOOD MUSSELS WITH DYNAMITE SAUCE

GRAPEFRUIT AND CHICKEN SALAD

KAFFIR LIME-ROASTED WHOLE SNAPPER WITH MANGO SALAD

SAMBAL KANG KONG

HOT AND SPICY FRIED FISH

MALAY MUSHROOM AND CASHEW CURRY

CHILLI BLACK BEAN NOODLES WITH SHIITAKE MUSHROOMS

soul soup with cockles and kick

I first tasted a version of this lunch soup cooked for me in the family kitchen of a friend in Ho Chi Minh City. Shopping with her in the cool of the morning in the local Thai Binh market almost every day over a month was a pure thrill for the senses, as were the market breakfasts of noodle and rice meal-in-a-bowl dishes.

Now I always have a clump of Vietnamese mint (also called rau ram, hot mint or laksa leaf) in my garden so I can make this. For those wanting to grow this hardy herb, ask for it at plant centres; it is from the Polygonaceae family and its botanical name is Persicaria odorata.

1kg fresh cockles in the shell
2 cups water
5 small tomatoes, halved, cores removed
¼ teaspoon freshly ground Szechwan peppercorns or black pepper
¼ teaspoon salt
½ teaspoon sugar
½ dried red chilli, crushed, or 1 fresh red chilli, sliced, to taste
leaves only of 1 bunch Vietnamese mint (about 1 cup)
½ bunch garlic chives, cut into 5cm lengths
1 block soft (silken) tofu, cut into 8 pieces

Rinse the cockles in cold water and scrub if necessary. Place the cleaned cockles in a pan with one cup of the water, cover with the lid and bring to the boil. Remove the cockles to a dish as they open. This takes only about 2–3 minutes. Turn the heat down to a simmer and add the tomatoes and seasonings with the second cup of water.

Remove the cockle meat from the shells with a teaspoon and set aside. Once the tomatoes have softened, drop in the herbs to wilt. Lower the tofu gently into the broth and return the cockle meat to the pan to heat through. You can also add chunks of fresh fish such as snapper or gurnard to poach at this stage if you want.

Ladle into 2 generous-sized bowls, breathe in deeply and wind down with this one!

SERVES 2

spicy basil chicken

This is so simple it barely needs a recipe. If you happen to have unexpected guests who call by for drinks and you want them to stay on for dinner, you can easily increase the quantities or extend it with another dish and some greens.

2 skinless chicken breasts
1 tablespoon chopped ginger
1 teaspoon sugar
1 teaspoon sesame oil
1 tablespoon light soy sauce
1–2 tablespoons vegetable oil
2 shallots, sliced
1 red chilli, sliced
2 tablespoons fish sauce
1 well-packed cup Thai sweet basil leaves

Cut the chicken breasts into strips and marinate with the ginger, sugar, sesame oil and soy sauce.

Heat the oil in a frying pan or wok and add the shallots. Cook until fragrant and then add the chicken breast. Stir-fry the chicken until golden, sprinkle with the chilli, fish sauce and basil leaves and toss well. Serve on steaming bowls of rice with vegetables.

SERVES 2 GENEROUSLY

hopping good mussels with dynamite sauce

Having discovered fresh New Zealand green-shell mussels here on a recent trip, my friends from Thai House cooking school in Bangkok used my stone mortar and pestle to produce a sweet, sour, hot and savoury sauce for serving with them.

24 mussels in shell
1 cup water
2 stalks lemon grass
5 kaffir lime leaves, torn
1 red chilli, sliced
**1 handful Thai sweet
 basil leaves**

Dynamite Sauce
**5 dynamite (bird's eye) chillies
 or milder long chillies**
5 cloves garlic
1 tablespoon lime juice
½ tablespoon white sugar
1 tablespoon fish sauce

Clean and de-beard mussels. Steam them in a large saucepan with water, crushed stalks of lemon grass, kaffir lime leaves, red chilli and some Thai sweet basil leaves if you have them. When the mussels open pile them and the flavourings (for good visual effect) into a large bowl and serve with plenty of the Dynamite Sauce.

Pound the dynamite chillies and garlic using a mortar and pestle, then add the lime juice, white sugar and fish sauce and stir to combine. Taste and adjust the heat, sourness, sweetness and saltiness to suit.

This is also good with fried fish, poached chicken or with duck. Crushed dried coriander seeds and white pepper can also be added.

I'd suggest making double or even triple the recipe, and if you don't have a mortar and pestle, you can do it all in a food processor.

SERVES 2

grapefruit and chicken salad

This Vietnamese salad is traditionally served with a side dish of crispy prawn crackers. A chopstickful of salad is placed on top of a cracker and they are eaten together. Pomelo can be substituted for the grapefruit if this is available. Pink grapefruit can also be used.

4 sweet grapefruit
⅓ telegraph cucumber
1 cooked chicken breast, shredded
1 red chilli, sliced
¼ cup coriander leaves
¼ cup Thai sweet basil leaves
¼ cup mint leaves
2 tablespoons lime juice
2 teaspoons sugar
1–2 teaspoons fish sauce
pinch of salt
pinch of freshly ground black pepper
2 tablespoons chopped roasted peanuts
2 tablespoons fried shallots
extra herbs for garnishing
fried prawn crackers for serving (optional)

Peel and remove the pith from the grapefruit. Use a small sharp knife to remove the segments into a plastic or stainless steel strainer placed over a bowl. Flick out any seeds and allow to drain. This will yield about 2 cups of flesh.

Cut the cucumber lengthwise, remove the seeds with a teaspoon and slice the flesh thinly. Place the chicken and cucumber into another bowl. Add the drained grapefruit, chilli, herbs and toss gently. Sprinkle with the lime juice, sugar, fish sauce and seasonings. Taste and adjust flavourings if required.

Pile the salad onto a large plate, sprinkle with the peanuts and shallots and garnish with herbs.

SERVES 2

kaffir lime-roasted whole snapper with mango salad

Although this recipe calls for a whole fish, if you don't fancy dealing with one then purchase some snapper fillets. Smother the fillets with the flavourings and roast briefly in a hot oven until the fish is just cooked. As they say throughout Asia — 'same, same' but different!

**1 whole fresh snapper,
  sufficient for 2 people**
6 kaffir lime leaves, torn
**1 thumb-sized piece ginger,
  peeled**
10cm piece lemon grass
**1 teaspoon crushed Szechwan
  peppercorns**
2 tablespoons light olive oil
¼ teaspoon salt
1 lime, quartered

Salad
1 ripe mango
½ red capsicum
½ orange or yellow capsicum
**1 cup cucumber ribbons (use
  a vegetable peeler to shave
  the cucumber into ribbons,
  discarding the middle with
  all the seeds)**
**¼ cup coarsely chopped
  coriander**
**½ cup mint or Thai basil leaves
  or a mixture**
2 teaspoons fish sauce
**juice and grated zest of
  1 orange**
**1 kaffir lime leaf, midrib
  removed, shredded**

Preheat the oven to 200°C. Pat the fish dry with a paper towel and make several criss-cross slashes on either side. Place in a small roasting dish or cast-iron pan lined with baking paper. Place the lime leaves, ginger, lemon grass and peppercorns into a mortar and mash with the pestle until bruised, to release the flavours. Mix in the oil and salt. Spoon some of the mixture into the cavity of the fish and the remainder under and over the fish. Squeeze the lime wedges over the fish and tuck a lime wedge into the cavity. Leave the other wedges alongside to roast. Allow to rest for 5–10 minutes while you prepare the salad.

Cut the cheeks off the mango and score the flesh with a knife in a criss-cross diamond pattern or fine slices, cutting towards the skin but not right through. Use a large tablespoon or knife to release the mango pieces into a bowl or dish. Remove the core and seeds from the capsicums and cut the flesh into chunks. Add the capsicums, cucumber and herbs and toss together gently with the mango. Sprinkle with the fish sauce, orange juice and zest and lime leaf and toss again to combine the flavours.

Roast the snapper for about 10 minutes or until the flesh has just lost its translucency. It should be tinged golden brown on the outside. Check for doneness by inserting a knife into the flesh — it should come away from the bones cleanly. Arrange the fish on a heated platter and serve with the salad. Spoon any juices from the roasting pan over the fish.

SERVES 2

sambal kang kong

This is a spicy Malay recipe for kang kong (water spinach), which is characterised by its hollow stems and slender spear-shaped leaves. It has an affinity for stronger flavours. This dish is flavoured with coconut cream, shrimp paste and chilli. It is a favourite of mine.

500g bunch water spinach
1 whole fresh red chilli, finely chopped
2 large shallots or ½ red onion, finely chopped
½ teaspoon shrimp paste (blachan), dry-roasted or you can use Lee Kum Kee fine shrimp paste
1 tablespoon vegetable oil
1–2 tablespoons coconut cream
salt for seasoning

Wash the water spinach well and trim away about 5–6cm off the ends to remove the tough part of the stalks. Cut the leaves from the stems and then either leave the stems whole or cut in half.

To make the sambal paste, pound the chilli, shallots and shrimp paste together using a mortar and pestle, or mix in a food processor until well blended.

Heat the oil in a frying pan, add the sambal paste and cook over a medium heat until it is fragrant. Add the prepared water spinach stems to the pan first as these will take a little longer to cook. Toss and then add the leaves. Allow the leaves to wilt down and toss again. Lastly pour in the coconut cream and season with salt to taste. Serve this dish to accompany meat or seafood dishes with plenty of hot jasmine rice.

SERVES 2 AS A SIDE DISH

Chilli heat: To remove some of the heat from chillies, cut the chilli lengthwise and use the tip of the knife to flick out the seeds and pare away some of the white membrane. Chop, slice or cut the flesh into slivers.

Shrimp paste: To dry roast, wrap in foil and place over a gas flame or in a hot oven until the paste is crumbly.

hot and spicy fried fish

I cook this whenever I can get hold of very fresh fish. It's one of the most enjoyable ways of eating your catch that I know of. I used to think fishing was like watching paint dry but the anticipation of cooking something I've caught myself has changed that! I'm working on beating my current record of a 5.9kg (13lb) snapper.

1 small whole flounder, sole or snapper
flour to coat
2 tablespoons peanut or vegetable oil
1 tablespoon salted black beans, rinsed and chopped
1 large clove garlic, chopped
1 tablespoon julienned ginger
2 ripe tomatoes, cored and quartered
1–2 tablespoons sweet chilli sauce (to taste)
1 tablespoon light soy sauce or ½ tablespoon fish sauce
¼ teaspoon ground Szechwan pepper
2 tablespoons chopped chives
coriander to garnish

Rinse the fish and pat dry with paper towels. Make 2–3 slashes on either side of the fish with a sharp knife. Place the flour into a large dish or plastic bag and lightly coat the fish with flour. Shake off excess.

Heat 1 tablespoon of the oil in a non-stick wok or large frying pan until hot. Lower the fish carefully into the wok or pan and reduce the heat to medium. Fry until the underside is golden before carefully turning over. I find it easier to turn the fish with the help of a wide-bladed spatula and some tongs tucked under the gills.

Cook the other side until golden and check that the fish is cooked by inserting a knife into the flesh. It should just come away from the bones. Transfer the fish to a warm serving dish.

Heat the remaining oil in the same pan and add the black beans, garlic and ginger. Toss these flavourings together, allowing them to sizzle until fragrant before adding the tomatoes and sweet chilli sauce. Simmer for about 2 minutes until the tomatoes have cooked through but are still holding their shape. Add the soy (or fish) sauce, pepper and chives and combine. Pour the tomato mixture over the fish and garnish with the coriander.

Serve hot with rice and stir-fried vegetables. Enough for 2, but this depends on the size of fish.

Variation: You can also coat whole small fish with the tempura beer batter (page 20) and serve these individually with the sauce. Keep cooked fish upright on a pan lined with paper towels in the oven while you fry the others.

malay mushroom and cashew curry

As a variation, add cubed lamb or chicken to the pan before adding the mushrooms. Allow to brown slightly and toss to coat the meat with the spice mixture.

250g Swiss brown or white button mushrooms
1–2 tablespoons vegetable oil
1 clove garlic, crushed
1 tablespoon finely chopped ginger
½ red onion, sliced
1 teaspoon ground cumin
1 red or green chilli, seeds removed, sliced
¼ teaspoon salt
½ cup milk
¼ teaspoon sugar
¼ cup roasted cashews, unsalted
¼ cup coconut cream
½ tablespoon shredded mint leaves

Slice the mushrooms thickly and set aside. In a deep frying pan, heat the oil on a medium heat and add the garlic, ginger and onion. Cook until the onion is golden in colour and soft. Sprinkle the cumin over and continue cooking until fragrant.

Add the mushrooms and chilli to the pan. Stir-fry for 2 minutes and season with salt. Stir in the milk and sugar and bring to the boil. Tip in the cashews. Reduce the heat and simmer for 3–4 minutes, stirring occasionally until the curry has thickened. Blend in the coconut cream and mint leaves. Taste and adjust the seasoning to suit. Serve this curry with steamed rice.

SERVES 2 AS A SIDE DISH

chilli black bean noodles with shiitake mushrooms

You choose your noodle, some colourful vegies and in about 10 minutes flat you will have a meal from scratch to share with your mate. And remember … if you want to live a long and happy life, never cut your noodles!

¼ **cup dried sliced shiitake mushrooms**
boiling water
1 teaspoon vegetable oil
½ **teaspoon sesame oil**
1 tablespoon ginger or 1 clove garlic, crushed
6 Brussels sprouts, quartered
½ **cup sliced green beans**
½ **red capsicum, cut into diamonds**
300g fresh noodles (or 2 servings prepared dried noodles such as udon, somen or egg noodles)
1 tablespoon minced black bean and garlic paste
1 fresh chilli, sliced, or 1 teaspoon chilli bean sauce
1 cup mung bean sprouts
¼ **cup coriander leaves or sliced spring onions**

Heat 2 dinner plates or noodle bowls. Soften the mushrooms by covering with boiling water as directed on page 47.

Heat the oils in a wok or heavy-based frying pan and add the ginger or garlic. Allow to sizzle and when fragrant add the vegetables and drained mushrooms. Stir-fry for 2 minutes, adding 1–2 tablespoons of reserved mushroom soaking water to moisten and create steam. This also helps the vegetables cook through quickly without scorching. Add the noodles to the wok or pan, then the seasonings. Toss evenly to mix through. Stir-fry for a further 2 minutes. Take off the heat and divide between the two dishes. Scatter the bean sprouts and herbs on top. This dish is just as good served at room temperature as a noodle salad.

Variations: Try adding ¼ cup shelled green prawns to the vegetable mixture. Squid or chicken would also work well with the basic recipe. To serve, top with freshly roasted peanuts, cashews or almonds and fried shallots.

Fresh shiitake mushrooms can be used if available. Ask for them in the produce section of the supermarket or look for them at markets or Asian food stores.

Notes: Minced black bean and garlic paste is readily available in jars as a prepared paste or you can make your own. Use 2 tablespoons preserved salted black beans rinsed in cold water and drained. Mash to a paste with 2 cloves garlic.

Rehydrating dried shiitake mushrooms (Chinese mushrooms): To rehydrate dried sliced shiitake mushrooms, place them in a bowl and cover with boiling water. Leave to soak for about 5 minutes or until soft. Reserve the soaking liquid and use for stock. Whole dried mushrooms will take about 10 minutes. Any woody stems need to be trimmed off before using. Drain and use in stir-fries, soups, noodle and rice dishes (even risotto) or in hotpot-style casseroles.

eating solo

When I cook for one, there is always enough for two. You never know when your luck might change and, if not, there will always be enough for second helpings or a snack later on.

GARLIC CHIVE AND GINGER BABY OMELETTES

5-MINUTE SOUPY NOODLES WITH ASIAN BITS

HAM OFF THE BONE AND BEAN FRIED RICE

CHIVE AND CORIANDER FRIED RICE

INSTANT CHILL ON NOODLES

SQUID AND SPRING VEGETABLES

SALT, PEPPER AND CHILLI PRAWNS

HOT SOUR PRAWN AND TOFU SOUP

ASIAN SAUSAGE RICE (LUP CHEONG FAN) WITH FRIED EGG AND CHOY SUM GREENS

LAZY LAKSA

garlic chive and ginger baby omelettes

These tasty omelettes take 5 minutes to make from 'go' and are more like a cross between a fritter and pan-fried herb cake. My mum does an equally good version of this with a herb mixture of chives, coriander and mint.

2 fresh eggs
1–2 tablespoons Ginger,
    Shallot and Chilli Sauce
    (see page 12)
1 teaspoon vegetable oil or
    light olive oil
½ cup chopped garlic chives
coriander to garnish

Whisk together the eggs and Ginger, Shallot and Chilli Sauce. Heat the oil and toss the garlic chives in it until just wilted and an intense green colour. Pour in the egg mixture and tilt the pan to coat. Lift the edges of the omelette as it cooks to allow uncooked egg to seep underneath. When the egg is just beginning to set, use a spatula to divide the mixture into 3 smaller omelettes or wedges and flip these over to cook the other side. Remove them to a warmed plate and garnish with coriander.

You can serve these as a quick snack as they are or stuff them into a toasted bap with some lettuce leaves. For something more substantial pile the omelettes on top of steamed jasmine rice with some simply cooked choy sum greens and a few slices of lup cheong sausage on the side (cook these in the rice pan at the same time!)

MAKES 3 BABY OMELETTES

Variation

Oyster and chive omelette: Add drained whole oysters to the pan with the chives. Cook only briefly.

5-minute soupy noodles with asian bits

5 small dried shiitake
  mushrooms
½ teaspoon Salt and Szechwan
  Pepper Mix (see page 13)
1 block rice vermicelli noodles
  or udon noodles
500ml boiling water
4–5 stems choy sum or 2 baby
  bok choy
1 tablespoon chilli black bean
  sauce
a few drops sesame oil
herbs such as coriander,
  Vietnamese mint or Thai
  sweet basil for serving

Rinse the dried mushrooms and place into a saucepan with the seasoning and noodles. (Somen or soba noodles, which are packaged in neat bundles, can also be used in place of rice vermicelli or udon noodles.)

Pour the boiling water over and bring the soup to the boil. Unravel the noodles with chopsticks. Cook for 2–3 minutes.

Wash and trim the greens, cutting the bok choy lengthwise if using these and drop into the pan. Cook for a further 1–2 minutes until the mushrooms and choy sum stems are tender. Spoon the noodles, mushrooms and choy sum into a large, deep bowl and toss with the sauce. Add 1–2 ladles of the hot stock, and drizzle the sesame oil over. Top with the herbs.

ham off the bone and bean fried rice

There is nothing like leftover festive ham as the basis for concocting a quick meal. Once you're tired of ham steaks and salad, try this. From chopping to being ready in a bowl this takes less than 10 minutes!

2 cups cold, cooked jasmine rice
1 tablespoon peanut oil
¼ teaspoon sesame oil
½ cup smoky ham, diced
6 beans, stringed, cut into 1cm
  lengths
½ red onion, chopped
½ teaspoon salt
¼ teaspoon Szechwan
  peppercorns, ground
1 tablespoon light soy sauce
1 tablespoon oyster sauce
1 egg

Separate any large lumps of rice with the back of a wooden spoon. Heat the oils in a wok or frying pan until hot and add the rice, ham, beans and onion. Toss to mix and stir-fry until the rice is hot, the ham lightly browned and fragrant and the onion has softened. Sprinkle the seasonings and sauces over and stir to mix. Push the rice to the sides of the pan, making a well in the centre. Break in the egg and stir with a spatula to slightly blend the white with the yolk. Fold through the rice mixture and toss until the egg is just cooked.

PLENTY FOR 1 DEEP BOWL OR 2 RICE BOWLS FULL

chive and coriander fried rice

1 teaspoon oil, e.g. sunflower,
  peanut, light olive (optional)
1 tablespoon Ginger, Shallot
  and Chilli Sauce
  (see page 12)
1 ½ cups cold cooked rice
¼ cup chopped garlic chives
1 teaspoon light soy sauce
1 egg
¼ cup coarsely chopped
  coriander

Heat the oil in a wok or frying pan until hot (if using a non-stick pan omit the oil). Add the Ginger, Shallot and Chilli Sauce, rice and chives. Toss to mix and stir-fry to heat through until hot. Sprinkle the soy sauce over and stir through. Push the rice to the sides of the pan, making a well in the centre. Break in the egg and stir with a spatula to slightly blend the white with the yolk. Fold through the rice mixture and toss until the egg is just cooked. Mix the coriander through and serve hot in bowls.

MAKES ENOUGH FOR 1 DEEP BOWL OR
2 RICE BOWLS FULL

instant chill on noodles

It's 4am. You're starving. Go forth with a packet of Nissin instant noodles. By the way, Nissin invented the instant noodle back in 1958 and it was voted the best invention of the century in Japan. Who came second? Sony Walkman!

1 packet Nissin
  instant noodles
1 egg
handful Thai sweet basil and
  laksa leaves
boiling water

Open the packet. Place the noodles and flavour sachets into a deep bowl. Break the egg in. Add the herbs. Pour boiling water over to cover. Place a dinner plate over the bowl and leave for 2 minutes. Whisk briefly with chopsticks. Eat.

When you can be bothered, the addition of a little miso paste and chopped chilli gives a kick to the dish.

squid and spring vegetables

This recipe is a reminder of a lunch dish I had while cruising through the beautiful limestone peaks in Halong Bay, a World Heritage Site in North Vietnam. It has flavours of the sea and its simplicity allows each ingredient to be a hero.

6–8 baby squid tubes
1 teaspoon Salt and Szechwan Pepper Mix (see page 13)
1 tablespoon fish sauce
1 teaspoon sugar
1 large ripe tomato
½ red onion
8–10 fresh asparagus spears
1 clove garlic
1 tablespoon vegetable oil
2 slices ginger, julienned
2 teaspoons light soy sauce
1 teaspoon Shao Hsing rice wine

Rinse the squid and pat dry with paper towels. Use a knife like a letter-opener down the side of each tube and open out flat. Score the inside flesh into diamonds, taking care not to cut right through. Place in a bowl with the seasoning, fish sauce and sugar and mix together.

Remove the core from the tomato and cut into wedges. Cut the onion into wedges and separate the layers. Slice the asparagus diagonally into long strips. Squash the garlic clove with the flat of a knife to release it from the papery skin. You want the garlic bruised and flattened so that it will release its flavour but not chopped so that it interferes with the dish.

Heat the oil with the ginger and garlic until just sizzling then add the onion. Stir-fry until the onion begins to soften, then add the squid and vegetables. Toss until the squid starts to curl up, add the soy sauce and wine and allow the juices to bubble up in the pan. Cook until the asparagus is crisp-tender. Serve in a shallow dish on top of a big scoop of rice or separately with a bowl of rice.

Adapt this dish easily for two by adding another side dish such as:
- Oyster and Chive Omelette (see page 50)
- Choy Sum (see page 24)

Or go totally soothing and gentle with tofu dressed with soy sauce, toasted sesame seeds and hot oil flavoured with chopped spring onion.

salt, pepper and chilli prawns

Treat yourself! Sometimes you need to make something really good and eat it all yourself … you don't always have to share. Chilli pepper squid is a popular take on the prawn version. Serve with plenty of Salt and Szechwan Pepper and wedges of lime.

Batter
½ **cup cornflour**
1 **egg**
⅓ **cup cold water**
pinch of salt

2 **cups vegetable oil**
450g **green prawns, shelled, deveined but tails left on**
2 **spring onions, diagonally sliced**
2 **cloves garlic, finely chopped**
2 **dried chillies, crushed**
3 **teaspoons Salt and Szechwan Pepper Mix (see page 13)**

Make the batter by mixing together the cornflour, egg, water and salt.

Heat the vegetable oil in a wok or saucepan until a cube of bread sizzles when dropped in, then coat each prawn with batter before dropping into the hot oil. Cook for about 4 minutes until golden and then remove with a slotted spoon and leave to drain on absorbent kitchen paper.

Pour the oil out of the wok leaving behind only 1 tablespoon. Reheat and then add the spring onions, garlic and chillies. Quickly stir-fry for 2 minutes and then return the prawns to the wok. Toss everything together quickly before sprinkling with the salt and peppercorns mix. Make sure everything is well mixed; serve piping hot.

Chilli pepper squid

Toss prepared squid in a hot oiled wok with Salt and Szechwan Pepper Mix, fresh chillies, finely chopped shallots and fresh coriander — great stuff!

hot sour prawn and tofu soup

Flavour is the key. A simple, one-pan scene-stealer. Choose a good quality brand of tom yum paste from the Asian section of your supermarket or from your local Asian grocery store.

3 dried shiitake mushrooms
375ml water
15cm piece lemon grass, split and bruised
1 kaffir lime leaf, midrib removed, shredded
2 slices ginger, julienned
1 tablespoon tom yum paste
½ block silken tofu
6 green prawns, shelled and deveined
1 tablespoon coriander leaves

Rinse the dried mushrooms and place in a saucepan with the water, lemon grass, kaffir lime leaf and ginger. Bring to the boil and simmer with the lid on for 5 minutes. Remove the softened mushrooms, trim the stems and cut each in half or into quarters if large. Put back in the pot.

Stir the tom yum paste into the stock until dissolved. Cut the tofu into 5 pieces. Add the tofu and prawns and simmer for a few minutes until the prawns are a bright coral colour. Ladle the soup into a bowl and garnish with the coriander.

asian sausage rice (lup cheong fan) with fried egg and choy sum greens

I eat solo some of the time and although I live by the rule that it's always good to indulge oneself when eating alone I don't necessarily want to go to great lengths.

This one-dish meal is just right. It combines several simple ingredients that I love to eat and it takes about 20 minutes, or as long as it takes for the rice to cook. If you are really feeling lazy then you could also steam the greens over the rice, but the fried egg on top is my weakness so I need to dirty a small pan for that.

1 cup jasmine rice
about 2 cups water
2 lup cheong
** (Chinese sausages)**
1 bunch/handful choy sum
** greens or 2 heads bok choy**
salt, to taste
vegetable oil
1 large free-range egg
condiments of your choice,
** such as light soy sauce,**
** oyster and chilli sauce**

Place the jasmine rice into a saucepan or the bowl of the rice cooker and wash under cold water several times until the water is clear. Pour in the water until it reaches the first joint of your middle finger or use the rule of thumb that works best for you using the absorption method. Level the top of the rice. Rinse the sausages and place on top of the rice. Bring the rice to the boil and when 'craters of the moon' appear on top of the rice, turn the heat down to the lowest setting and allow the rice to steam through for 10 minutes, covered.

Steam the greens on top of the rice, or heat about 2 cups of water in a saucepan and season with salt. When the water comes to the boil, blanch the greens until tender, then drain.

Remove the sausages from the pan and slice thinly on the diagonal. Spoon a large scoop of rice into the centre of a deep dish or bowl. Arrange the greens around the side and scatter the sausage over the top of the rice.

Heat a small frying pan with a little oil or use a non-stick pan, fry the egg to your liking and tip into the filled dish. Drizzle with the sauce that you want and eat with chopsticks and a spoon.

The fried egg on top is my weakness.

lazy laksa

Slippery, crunchy, creamy and spicy, and no pounding of paste. This hits the spot.

**1 cup cooked rice vermicelli or
   fresh hokkien noodles or
   ½ cup of each
boiling water
1 cup mung bean sprouts
1 teaspoon vegetable oil
¼ cup good quality laksa paste
¼ cup coconut milk
¾ cup water
3 deep-fried tofu puffs,
   quartered
½ cup sliced cooked chicken
   (about ½ chicken breast)
2–3 green prawns, shelled,
   deveined but tails left on
¼ cup sliced green beans
1 tablespoon each Vietnamese
   mint (laksa leaf), coriander
   and Thai sweet basil
½ red chilli, sliced
kaffir lime leaf, finely
   shredded, or lime zest
extra herbs and bean sprouts
   to garnish**

Place the noodles in a deep serving bowl and pour boiling water over to cover. Leave for 10 seconds, swish the noodles around with chopsticks and then drain off the water. Nip any ragged ends off the bean sprouts and place on top of the noodles.

Heat the oil in a wok or saucepan until hot, add the laksa paste and fry until fragrant and slightly thickened. Pour in the coconut milk and water, blending well. Add the remaining ingredients, except for the garnish. Bring to the boil and then reduce the heat to a simmer. Cook for 1 minute. Ladle the soup and bits over the noodles and bean sprouts. Garnish with the extra herbs and sprouts and serve with chopsticks and a spoon. Good to eat in front of the telly.

This recipe multiplies up easily. You can also add blachan (Malay shrimp paste) if you want.

for kids

We ate really well as kids. Maybe it was just because we were lucky to have parents who enjoyed great food. Hostel food at Uni was hell, but the food parcels from home were legendary.

CRISPY CHAR SIEU BAU (BARBECUE PORK BUNS)

CHICKEN AND MUSHROOM YAKATORI

LUP CHEONG SAUSAGE ROLLS

POT-STICKER DUMPLINGS

PORK AND CORIANDER STUFFED MUSHROOMS

GINGERY BEANY BEEF, PEAS
AND TUBULAR PASTA

SANG CHOY BAU (LETTUCE BUNS)

HOISIN SPUDS AND BACON

crispy char sieu bau (barbecue pork buns)

Char sieu is the Chinese barbecue pork with the appearance of red lacquer. It is often seen hanging in barbecue shop windows. Steamed barbecue pork buns are yeast breads with an enclosed pork filling. They are available fresh from Asian supermarkets, or in the deli section or freezer of some ordinary supermarkets.

**6 barbecue pork buns
    (fresh or frozen)
boiling water
2 tablespoons vegetable oil
sweet chilli sauce (optional)**

Place the buns into a largish steamer and place over boiling water. Steam, covered, for 10–15 minutes, longer if frozen. Remove from the steamer and peel off the paper liner from the underside of the buns.

Heat the oil in a large, non-stick frying pan and place the buns into the pan, tops facing down. Press down with a spatula to flatten slightly. Cook over a medium heat until golden brown and crispy before turning. Brown the underside. Serve hot with a side of sweet chilli sauce for dipping if the kids like this. The big kids definitely will.

SERVES 6

chicken and mushroom yakatori

Yakatori are popular Japanese grilled snacks usually served with drinks. Typical are skewered chicken with spring onion or chicken balls made with minced chicken brushed with yakatori sauce made from mirin, dark soy sauce, sake and sugar.

2 large (300g) chicken thigh fillets
bamboo skewers
250g Swiss brown or white button mushrooms
seven spice powder (optional)

Yakatori Marinade
1 tablespoon mirin
1 tablespoon sake
1 tablespoon dark soy sauce
2 teaspoons sugar

Cut each thigh fillet into about 9 cubes. Mix the marinade ingredients in a bowl and add the chicken. Marinate for 10–15 minutes or leave in the refrigerator until ready to use. Place the bamboo skewers in cold water to soak.

Preheat the grill to 200–220°C. Thread about 3 button mushrooms and 3 pieces of chicken alternately onto each skewer. Place the skewers on a foil-lined baking tray. Brush the chicken and mushrooms with yakatori marinade and place under a hot grill. Cook until the chicken is golden brown, basting each skewer with marinade during cooking. Turn the skewers once during cooking and brush with marinade as before. The chicken is cooked when the juices run clear when the meat is pierced with the point of a knife. Serve immediately. Sprinkle with seven spice powder if you wish.

MAKES 6 SKEWERS

lup cheong sausage rolls

Not for me ordinary sandwiches! As well as these, we loved egg foo young sandwiches.

8 Chinese lup cheong sausages
boiling water
8 slices of quality white
   sandwich loaf
8 iceberg or cos lettuce leaves

Place the sausages in a steamer and place over boiling water. Steam for 10–15 minutes until the sausages are tender. Cool.

Alternatively, you can steam the sausages on top of rice if you happen to be cooking rice the night before.

Lay the slices of bread on the bench. Place a lettuce leaf over each slice of bread, tearing the leaves if very large, but it doesn't really matter if they hang off the edges. Place a sausage along one edge and roll up firmly. Wrap 2 rolls per parcel in waxed kitchen paper and send off to school with a chilled pottle of fresh tropical fruit cut into chunks. Beware of lunch thieves!

These sandwiches can also be made with small baguettes or ficelle rolls. The sausages can be sliced diagonally, but they are better to eat whole.

Chinatown pork or Chinese barbecue pork is also a good substitute for sausage in these rolls.

SERVES 4

Mum always made sure our

lunches were worth stealing.

pot-sticker dumplings

You can cheat and buy these from an Asian grocery store, but they don't take long to make and are immensely satisfying to eat. Browning them in the pan before a quick simmering to cook them through gives them their unique appeal.

250g minced chicken or pork
½ cup chopped garlic chives
¼ cup finely chopped water chestnuts
1 tablespoon minced garlic
1 tablespoon minced ginger
½ teaspoon salt
½ teaspoon Szechwan or black pepper
24 gow gee wrappers
cold water
2 tablespoons vegetable oil
Chinese black vinegar or light soy sauce for serving

Mix the chicken or pork together with the next 6 ingredients in a bowl. Separate the gow gee wrappers and place them on a clean bench. Place a heaped teaspoon of filling into the centre of each wrapper. Wet the edge of the top half of the wrapper with cold water and fold up the bottom edge to enclose the filling. Lift each dumpling and sit it on its folded edge so that it resembles a purse with a base and 2 sides. You can freeze them on a flat tray or baking sheet at this stage if you want to have some on hand for emergencies, so it's a good idea if you have time to double or triple the recipe.

Heat the oil in a deep frying pan and when hot lower the dumplings into the pan. Turn the heat to medium and cook the base and both sides of the dumplings until golden brown. Carefully pour about 1cm of water into the pan, cover with the lid and allow the dumplings to cook for about 2 minutes before removing the lid. Allow all the moisture to evaporate. The dumplings should be cooked through and the wrappers tender and not soggy. You can allow them to crisp up slightly if you want to. Remove from the pan to a plate and serve with a small dipping bowl or dish of black vinegar or soy sauce.

MAKES 24

Note: Gow gee wrappers are round dumpling wrappers made from wheat flour and water. They are available either chilled or frozen. Dumplings can be steamed, poached or fried.

pork and coriander stuffed mushrooms

When we were growing up, we'd pester Mum to make these for us. They are also great lightly floured, dipped in batter and deep-fried until crispy and golden. Grown-ups seem to like them too.

8 medium-sized portobello mushrooms
250g minced pork
1 clove garlic, minced
1 tablespoon finely chopped ginger
2 tablespoons chopped coriander
1 spring onion, white part only, finely chopped
¼ teaspoon salt
¼ teaspoon sugar
pinch Szechwan or black pepper
2 teaspoons light soy sauce
2 teaspoons oyster sauce
2 teaspoons cornflour
1 teaspoon vegetable oil
1–2 tablespoons cold water

Trim the stems off the mushrooms. Mix together the pork, flavourings and cornflour in a bowl. Fill the mushroom caps using 2 tablespoons of mixture for each. Press the pork mixture gently into the mushrooms and smooth with the back of a spoon.

Heat the oil until hot in a large frying pan or wok. Place the mushrooms stuffing side down into the pan and cook until the pork is golden brown. Turn the mushrooms over to cook the other side. When the caps are browned, add the water to the pan but do not pour it directly over the mushrooms. Cover the pan briefly to ensure the mushrooms and filling cook through. Transfer to a warm dish, spoon any juices from the pan over. Serve with rice and vegetables.

SERVES 4

gingery beany beef, peas and tubular pasta

Macaroni cheese just doesn't come close to this. It is essentially a quick pasta dish with Asian flavours. Children will love the familiarity of the pasta shapes and the sweetness of the baby peas.

**1 cup rigati or other tubular
    pasta, such as macaroni**
1 teaspoon salt
½ cup frozen baby peas
1 small lean beef steak
**1 teaspoon cornflour blended
    with ¼ cup water**

Marinade
1 teaspoon dark soy sauce
**1 teaspoon black bean and
    garlic sauce**
**pinch of ground Szechwan
    peppercorns**
**1 tablespoon shredded ginger,
    julienned**
1 teaspoon peanut oil

Bring a saucepan of water to the boil, add the pasta and salt and cook according to packet directions. Add the peas to the pan just before the pasta is cooked through and bring back to the boil. Reserving 1–2 tablespoons of the cooking liquid, drain the pasta and peas into a colander and then tip back into the saucepan to keep hot.

Slice the beef steak across the grain into strips and place in a bowl. Add the marinade ingredients and toss to coat the beef. Heat a non-stick wok or frying pan until hot and fry the meat until browned on both sides and cooked to your liking. Tip the pasta and peas into the pan and mix together. Make a well in the centre of the pan, add the cornflour and water mixture and bring to the boil. Allow the sauce to thicken slightly, enough to coat the pasta. Serve hot in deep bowls.

SERVES 2–3

sang choy bau (lettuce buns)

This is one of those great recipes where once you have done all the slicing and cutting it only takes minutes to put together. Bursting with flavour and texture, it's a cunning way of adding more vegetables to the diet! Kids (and grown-ups) like helping themselves and wrapping up the parcels.

1 iceberg or cos lettuce
6–8 fresh shiitake or dried Chinese mushrooms
4 fresh wood ear mushrooms
1 small bundle bean thread vermicelli or glass noodles
1 recipe Asian Noodle Dressing (see page 11)
1 tablespoon peanut oil or vegetable oil
a few drops sesame oil
1 tablespoon Ginger, Shallot and Chilli Sauce (see page 12, but omit the chilli)
4 Chinese sausages (lup cheong), cooked and sliced
1 carrot, julienned
1 handful beans, snow peas or sugar snaps, sliced diagonally
1 red capsicum, sliced
1 cup mung bean sprouts
2 teaspoons soy sauce
fresh roasted peanuts (optional)

Separate and wash the lettuce leaves, drain well, place in a plastic bag, seal and chill. Rinse the mushrooms, place in a heatproof bowl and pour boiling water over them to cover. Stand for about 30 minutes or until softened. Meanwhile, soak the vermicelli in hot water until soft, and prepare the noodle dressing, leaving the herbs aside.

Once the dried mushrooms are ready to use, trim off the stems and any hard parts from the wood ear and slice. Heat the oils until hot, then add the sauce, Chinese sausage, carrot, beans, capsicum and the prepared mushrooms. Stir-fry for 2 minutes then add the sprouts, drained vermicelli and soy sauce. Toss until the sprouts are just wilted but still crisp. Remove from the heat.

Toss the dressing and the herbs through the filling and transfer to a serving bowl. Serve warm or cool with a small bowl of roasted peanuts to sprinkle on top. Allow diners to serve themselves by spooning the mixture into the chilled lettuce cups, then wrap and eat!

SERVES 4

Note: Wood ear mushrooms have a velvety texture almost like sea kelp. They are brown and grow in ear shapes. They have little flavour but are widely used in Asian cooking for their texture and visual qualities. Cut into thin strips and add to soups, stir-fries, sauces and casseroles towards the end of cooking. Dried wood ear need to be soaked in warm water until softened before using.

hoisin spuds and bacon

Every mother has a different version of this children's favourite and this is mine. It transports the humble potato from its Irish origins to the Asian table. Try this dish cold as a potato salad or stuffed into crisp iceberg or cos lettuce leaves.

3 large floury potatoes (such as Agria)
1 slice bacon 1cm thick
2 tablespoons hoisin sauce
1 tablespoon oyster sauce
freshly ground Szechwan pepper or black pepper
1 ½ cups water

Scrub the potatoes clean but don't peel them. Cut into largish chunks. Cut the bacon into thick strips or rectangles.

Heat a deep-sided non-stick frying pan until hot and stir-fry the bacon until golden brown. Add the potatoes, sauces and pepper and toss together for 1 minute.

Pour the water over the potatoes and bring to the boil. Cover with a lid and lower the heat to a simmer. The potatoes should be cooked through in about 15 minutes and only a couple of tablespoons of liquid should remain at the base of the pan.

SERVES 3–4 WITH RICE AND VEGETABLES

for comfort

There are some dishes that just sing 'chill out'. It's the sort of food that we like to serve up, kick off our shoes, put on some cruisy music and enjoy. It's always alluring because it's got that 'out of Mum's kitchen' feel about it — simple, soothing, nurturing.

YIN AND YANG CHICKEN

SOY POACHED CHICKEN BREAST

GINGER CHICKEN

TOFU WITH SPICY PORK AND MUSHROOM SAUCE

SOY AND STAR ANISE SLOW-COOKED PORK HOCK

RED DUCK CURRY

DEEP-FRIED TOFU IN AMBER BROTH

PHO BO (VIETNAMESE BEEF NOODLE SOUP)

SPICED BEEF STOCK

CONGEE (SAVOURY RICE PORRIDGE)

SEAFOOD AND MUSHROOM CUSTARD POTS

TOASTED BLACK SESAME PUDDING

SOY MILK CUSTARDS WITH GINGER SYRUP AND SPICED FRUIT

GINGER AND LEMON GRASS SYRUP

FIVE SPICE ROASTED PINEAPPLE AND MANGO

So get the cooking

over with … and couch out.

yin and yang chicken

Asian flavour — pure but not innocent. The recipes for Soy Poached Chicken Breast, and Ginger Chicken (see page 80) are simple pleasures on their own but dramatic if served together, if you want to serve a platter of succulent chicken for a crowd. I generally get everything ready in two separate saucepans, using chicken breasts for both recipes. The yin and yang aspects come together either on individual plates or on a large round platter. You can slice each breast into 2 lengthwise to make serving easier. Arrange the soy chicken and the ginger chicken together in the shape of a yin and yang symbol. Serve the dark sauce and the light ginger broth in jugs to pass separately.

soy poached chicken breast

4 large fresh chicken breasts
8 slices ginger
1 bottle (410ml) prepared
 chicken marinade
2 whole star anise
1 teaspoon Szechwan
 peppercorns
2 spring onions, knotted
cold water
fresh coriander to garnish

Trim any fat from the chicken breasts. Rinse and pat dry. Place the chicken and the remaining ingredients, except the water and coriander, into a large saucepan. Add sufficient water to cover the chicken. Bring to a simmer, cover the pan and cook for about 20 minutes, until the chicken juices run clear when the flesh is pierced. Transfer the chicken from the pan to a warm plate, allow to rest for 5–10 minutes to firm up the meat. Cut into Asian-style pieces (about 2cm-thick slices).

Serve with chopped fresh coriander and the cooking juices poured over and accompany with plenty of steamed jasmine rice.

SERVES 4

Notes

1. The ready-made chicken marinade can be substituted with ¾ cup each light and dark soy sauce, ¼ cup Shao Hsing rice wine and 2 tablespoons honey. Stir to combine.
2. The poaching liquid can be reused several times if you simply allow it to cool and freeze it in a plastic tub. The flavour intensifies each time it is used.

yin and yang chicken

ginger chicken

This Asian-style cooked chicken is gently flavoured with ginger and the poaching method ensures the meat is tender and juicy.

**1.5kg whole fresh chicken or
4 large chicken breasts
1 spring onion
8 thick slices fresh ginger
1 teaspoon salt
8 stalks coriander
1 tablespoon Szechwan
peppercorns
8 cups boiling water
fresh coriander to garnish**

Wash the chicken and dry it with paper towels. Tuck the wings under and across the back. Coil the spring onion and place it in the cavity with 4 slices of the ginger. Rub the chicken with salt.

Twist the coriander stalks into a knot and place in a saucepan large enough to hold the chicken submerged in poaching liquid. Add the peppercorns and remaining ginger and pour the boiling water over. Lower the chicken, breast side down, into the pan and bring the water back to the boil. Reduce to a simmer, cover, and cook for exactly 25 minutes for a whole chicken, 15–20 minutes for chicken breasts. Turn off the heat, keep the lid on and allow the chicken to poach for 40 minutes (30 minutes for chicken breasts).

Lift out the chicken and drain. Cut into Asian-style pieces and garnish with fresh coriander. Serve with Ginger, Shallot and Chilli Sauce (see page 12), steamed rice and lightly cooked bok choy or choy sum.

SERVES 4

tofu with spicy pork and mushroom sauce

This comfort dish is probably best described as the Chinese version of spaghetti Bolognese. If you haven't been too sure about tofu in the past, you'll be hooked after this! Straw mushrooms and the sauces used here can be found in the Asian section of most supermarkets. Look for dried Chinese mushrooms at your Asian grocery store. Fresh shiitake mushrooms can be used, although these have a much milder flavour.

8 dried Chinese mushrooms or ½ cup drained straw mushrooms
500g fresh, soft tofu
2 tablespoons peanut or vegetable oil
2 cloves garlic, crushed
2 tablespoons grated fresh ginger
1 large shallot, peeled and sliced
1 red chilli, seeds removed, finely sliced
300g lean minced pork
1–2 teaspoons chilli bean sauce
1 tablespoon black bean sauce
1 tablespoon light soy sauce
1 tablespoon cornflour mixed with ¼ cup cold water
½ cup chopped fresh coriander

Soak the Chinese mushrooms in hot water for 30 minutes until softened then drain. Remove the stems, slice and set aside. If using straw mushrooms, cut these in half. Cut the tofu into 2cm cubes and drain on paper towels.

Heat the oil in a large frying pan or wok until hot. Add the garlic, ginger, shallot and chilli and stir-fry until fragrant. Add the pork and stir-fry for 5 minutes or until the meat is cooked through. Stir in the mushrooms and sauces, cook for a further 2 minutes, then blend in the cornflour and water mixture. When the sauce has thickened, slip the tofu into the pan and heat through, spooning the sauce gently over to coat the tofu. Sprinkle with the coriander.

Spoon the tofu and sauce into deep bowls and serve with rice and lightly cooked Chinese greens.

SERVES 4

... slow and slinky

I have sneaked in this single slow dish as even though we often race through the week some of us might find comfort in mooching around in the kitchen for a bit. For me it's a way to wind down. This is also one dish that has allowed me to take residence in other people's kitchens because it is just sooo good!

soy and star anise slow-cooked pork hock

This is how to create a sensational cool-weather meal using a very economical and much-forgotten cut of pork — the hock. Belly pork is equally good cooked this way. The resulting dish is succulent and fragrant. Once cooked the meat is so tender that it can be cut with a spoon. But best of all is the sticky, savoury-sweet pork skin. Absolutely delicious.

2 (about 900g–1kg each) whole fresh pork hocks
¼ cup dark soy sauce
4 tablespoons sugar
4 teaspoons salt
¼ cup vegetable oil

Fragrant Stock
10 slices fresh ginger
10 cloves garlic, peeled and bruised
10 shallots, peeled
4 whole star anise
2 cinnamon sticks
½ cup crushed yellow rock sugar
2 tablespoons garlic and black bean sauce
⅔ cup dark soy sauce
½ cup Shao Hsing rice wine
1 litre chicken stock

To finish:
2 golden kumara, peeled
coriander to garnish

Blanch the pork hocks in boiling water. Discard the water and rinse the hocks under cold running water. Pat dry with paper towels. Mix the soy sauce, sugar and salt together in a large bowl and place the pork in the marinade for 20–30 minutes. Spoon the marinade over the hocks and turn several times to ensure they are evenly coated.

Heat the oil in a large saucepan or stock pot and brown the hocks all over, turning carefully with tongs. Add the ginger, garlic and shallots and fry until fragrant. Add the remaining stock ingredients. Cover, bring to the boil, then reduce the heat. Simmer gently for 2 hours, turning the hocks over after an hour to ensure they are evenly glazed and cooked.

Cut the kumara into thick rounds and add to the pan. Cook for a further 15–20 minutes. The meat should be very soft and the kumara cooked. Transfer the pork and kumara to a warmed serving dish and spoon the fragrant stock over. Garnish with coarsely chopped coriander.

SERVES 4 WITH RICE AND ASIAN GREENS

Note: Star anise has a robust licorice aroma so it pays not to be heavy handed. Star anise marries well with slow-cooked dishes, beef, pork, five spice, ginger, shallots, spring onions, mandarin or any citrus peels and Szechwan peppercorns. Yellow rock sugar gives a glossier finish to the glaze. Available from Asian food stores and some supermarkets.

red duck curry

This is traditionally made using a whole barbecue-roasted duck from the Asian deli, cut up in pieces with bones and all, but I like to make it with just the duck breasts and thigh meat for really lazy eating. Use the rest of the duck and the bones for noodle soup if there is anything left on the carcass.

1 whole roast duck
1 teaspoon vegetable oil
210g jar Valcom Red Curry Paste or ½ cup other good-quality red curry paste
400ml coconut milk
6 tablespoons shaved palm sugar
4 tablespoons fish sauce
15 kaffir lime leaves
3 tomatoes, cored and quartered
½ cup Thai sweet basil leaves

Use kitchen scissors/shears to cut down either side of the back-bone and remove. (This sounds like hard work, but only takes about 5 minutes.) Cut the roast duck into about 6 portions — 2 breasts, 2 leg and thighs, and meat from the wing portions. You can leave the legs as whole drumsticks if you wish or remove the leg bone if you choose to or have time. Cut the breast and thigh meat into 2cm-thick pieces. Set aside.

Heat the oil in a large pan — I use a wok or a heavy risotto-type pan with deep sides so that the meat is in a single layer. Add the curry paste to the pan and fry until the paste starts to bubble up. It will spit slightly so stand clear or use a splatter guard! Fry for about 1 minute until fragrant. Add the coconut milk, palm sugar and fish sauce. Simmer for 5 minutes, stirring to dissolve the sugar.

Take 10 of the kaffir lime leaves and fold these along the midrib until the segments of the leaf break and tear along the rib. Remove the rib by holding the stem end and ripping the leaf away from it. Add these leaves to the curry. Scrunch the remaining whole leaves in the palm of your hand to release the aromatic oils and add to the pan (these are for flavour and looks). Lower the duck into the curry sauce and scatter the tomatoes on top. Simmer gently for another 10 minutes. Ladle the liquid over the duck several times to keep it moistened.

Spoon the duck curry into a large serving dish. Sprinkle the basil leaves over and serve hot with jasmine rice and perhaps some thinly sliced fresh pineapple and shredded mint leaves.

SERVES 4

deep-fried tofu in amber broth

This recipe has been adapted from my soy-splattered Japanese cookbook. I've lightened the sauce, taken out the thickening and doubled the quantity of tofu as I always manage to greedily eat a couple of pieces before it gets to the table! The tofu is crispy and tender on the outside but still creamy on the inside. Do not use a pressed tofu as the texture will be too firm and dry.

2 blocks (2 x 300g) tofu
about 500ml vegetable oil
for deep-frying
cornflour

Amber Broth
2 cups dashi (bonito) stock
(see opposite)
5 tablespoons light soy sauce
5 tablespoons mirin
¼ cup (5g sachet) bonito flakes
1 tablespoon ginger juice
(see below)

For serving:
3 tablespoons finely grated
ginger
3 tablespoons grated
daikon radish
2 spring onions, finely sliced
¾ cup bonito threads or flakes

Cut each block of tofu into 6 pieces. Place on paper towels to remove some of the moisture. Pat dry. Heat the oil in a wok or deep-sided pan. Tip some cornflour into a dish, lightly coat each piece of tofu and pat off the excess. Deep-fry the tofu in batches until light golden brown. Drain on paper towels and keep warm.

In a saucepan, combine the stock, soy sauce and mirin and bring to the boil. Add the bonito flakes and take off the heat. Strain the broth through a sieve lined with a paper towel and placed over a jug, then pour back into the pan. Add the ginger juice and bring back to the boil, then take off the heat. The broth should be clear and slightly reduced.

Place pieces of fried tofu in small bowls or shallow dishes. Spoon some ginger, radish and spring onion alongside the tofu. Carefully pour about 3–4 tablespoons of broth into each bowl. Sprinkle the bonito threads or flakes over the tofu. Eat with chopsticks.

SERVES 4–6

Ginger Juice: Place finely grated ginger onto a small square of clean muslin or a heavy paper towel and squeeze over a small bowl to extract the juice.

Dashi Stock: Use either an instant dashi stock or prepare using
1 (about 80g) piece of konbu, wiped with a damp cloth and
placed in 2 ¼ cups water. Konbu is a dark green/brown kelp sold
in oblong sheets. Heat without boiling until the konbu is
softened and feels spongy. Remove from the water and add
5g bonito flakes. Bring to the boil and then take off the heat.
Allow the bonito flakes to settle to the bottom of the pan and
then strain the stock through a paper towel placed over a sieve.

pho bo (vietnamese beef noodle soup)

There are many versions of pho bo soup and my first experience of this was many years ago in my Aunty Helen's kitchen in Hong Kong. Originating from North Vietnam and called 'pot au feu annamite' by the French colonists, it is served for breakfast or lunch at market and street stalls and family-owned cafés in Hanoi that specialise in pho (soup — bo is beef). It also referred to as Pho Hanoi. The secret is in the stock. With the zing of limes, the heat of chilli and the freshness of herbs countering the silken noodles and the crunch from bean sprouts, pho is the perfect balance of flavour, aroma and texture.

For serving:

**1 recipe Spiced Beef Stock
(see page 90)**
500g fresh rice noodles
**500g sirloin steak, very
thinly sliced**
1 small onion, thinly sliced
**2 spring onions, finely sliced
on the diagonal**

Accompaniments

**mung bean sprouts, rinsed,
drained and trimmed**
sprigs of coriander
Thai sweet basil leaves
**coriander, or thorny coriander,
torn, if available**
Vietnamese mint
lime wedges
fresh red chillies, finely sliced
fish sauce in a small dish
freshly ground black pepper

Bring the beef stock to the boil in a large saucepan. Place the rice noodles in a heatproof bowl and pour boiling water over them to heat through. Drain these well and divide them between 6 deep noodle soup bowls.

Place a portion of sliced beef steak, onion and spring onions into each bowl. Pour 2–3 ladles of hot stock over the toppings. The thinly sliced beef will cook in the heat of the hot broth and should be pink and very tender.

Serve with the accompaniments arranged on a large platter, allowing everyone to add their own choice of herbs, some bean sprouts, a squeeze of lime and other seasonings.

MAKES 6 GENEROUS SERVES

To slice beef thinly: Wrap it in plastic food wrap and place in the freezer for about an hour, then it will be easier to slice very thinly. Allow the beef to thaw completely before using.

Note: Thorny coriander (eryngo or saw tooth herb) has long blades with serrated edges. It has a milder flavour than normal coriander and is used torn into soups and salads.

spiced beef stock

Traditionally this stock is made the day before with beef shin bones or oxtail along with a piece of beef brisket, then strained and refrigerated. If you don't have time, a good quality ready-made beef stock can be used instead. Infused with the distinctive spice flavours of ginger, cinnamon, star anise, fennel and cloves, the final broth has a dimension of its own.

2 litres quality beef stock
1 litre water
1 thumb-sized piece ginger, peeled
1 onion, sliced
3 whole star anise
1 cinnamon stick
1 large bay leaf
2 whole cloves
1 teaspoon fennel seeds
1 walnut-sized piece yellow rock sugar or 1 tablespoon sugar
1 tablespoon fish sauce

Measure the beef stock and water into a large saucepan. Using tongs hold the ginger over a gas flame or under a hot grill and char it all over. Rinse any loose ash from the ginger. Bruise the knob of ginger with a heavy pestle or rolling pin. Add the ginger and the rest of the stock ingredients to the pan and bring to the boil. Lower the heat and simmer the stock for 30 minutes. Allow to cool and then strain into a large bowl or jug. Cover with plastic food wrap and refrigerate until ready to use. The stock will keep for 2–3 days if kept chilled or it can be frozen in plastic containers for later use.

MAKES ABOUT 2.5 LITRES

Noodles. Pure and simple in a bowl of hot broth. Nurturing. Silken. Slippery. The big easy.

congee (savoury rice porridge)

Comfort — slippers — couch. Sometimes we don't want to be too challenged. Whether it's called jook, cháo or congee, this is the ultimate comfort dish for Asians throughout the world. A simple, plain congee is one of the first foods that Asians give to their young infants. Although congee needs a bit of slow cooking, the amount of effort is minimal. Scented with chicken broth and ginger, it instantly holds appeal for grownups — as a soothing dish any time of the day. It's also a proven hangover cure!

½ **cup jasmine rice**
½ **teaspoon salt**
½ **teaspoon peanut or vegetable oil**
¼ **cup dried prawns or shrimps, rinsed (optional)**
1 litre water
1 litre chicken stock
1 tablespoon finely shredded ginger

Place the rice into a sieve and wash it until the water runs clear. Drain and tip the rice into a medium-sized saucepan. Mix in the salt and oil, then add the dried prawns or shrimps. Cover with the water and allow to soak for 1 hour.

Measure in the chicken stock, add the ginger and bring to the boil. Reduce the heat and simmer for 1 hour, stirring occasionally to stop the congee from catching on the base of the pan — a smoky flavour is not what you want!

Toppings and condiments

Try pickled vegetables, fermented bean curd, cooked mussels, shredded cooked chicken, Asian roast duck, slices of marinated firm-fleshed fish, boiled salted duck egg, steamed thousand year egg, fried 'baguette' savoury doughnuts cut into 2cm lengths, coriander leaves, chopped chives or spring onions, light soy sauce, white pepper. Another option is to try adding meat floss, which is salted dried meat like jerky, that has been very carefully teased so that the meat fibres resemble fluffy floss. Try cuttle fish or pork floss.

For serving: Place small dishes of a choice of toppings, herbs and condiments onto a tray or platter. Spoon the hot congee into bowls and let each person help themselves from the platter.

seafood and mushroom custard pots

100g green, shelled prawns
100g scallops
4 portobello mushrooms or shiitake mushrooms, sliced
1 ½ teaspoons grated ginger (optional)
½ teaspoon sesame oil
1 teaspoon light soy sauce
1 cup cooked spinach or watercress, drained and chopped

Custard
2 cups dashi stock, cooled (see page 87)
4 eggs
1 tablespoon mirin
¼ teaspoon salt
sliced spring onion to garnish

Combine the seafood, mushrooms, ginger if using, oil and soy sauce in a bowl. Marinate for 15–20 minutes. Divide the spinach between 6 cups or small bowls (125–150ml capacity). Spoon the seafood mixture into the cups, dividing evenly. Place a whole prawn or scallop and a slice of mushroom on top of each cup.

For the custard, whisk together the dashi, eggs, mirin and salt. Strain into the cups and then cover each cup with foil. Place the cups in a large steamer over boiling water. Cover and steam over a medium heat for 10–12 minutes or until the custard is just set. Remove the foil and sprinkle with spring onion. Serve hot or cooled and eat with a spoon.

SERVES 6

toasted black sesame pudding

Glossy, black and served hot or warm, this slightly mysterious-looking sweet is as dark as licorice. As it cooks the fragrance of toasted sesame pervades the kitchen. Chinese mothers believe it promotes a fine complexion with a healthy glow.

Black Sesame Paste
1 packet (about 227g) black sesame seeds
cold water

Pudding
4 Chinese soup spoons or ⅓ cup black sesame paste
2 Chinese soup spoons or 3 tablespoons fine rice flour
extra cold water
3 sticks or 200g brown sugar slab
coconut cream and toasted white sesame seeds for serving (optional)

Tip the sesame seeds into a large non-stick pan. Pick over if necessary to remove any husks or stalks. Toast the seeds over a medium heat until fragrant, swirling occasionally to ensure they toast evenly and do not burn. Allow to cool. Transfer the seeds to a blender and add a cup of water to start the blending process. Gradually add more water and blend until the paste is the thickness of creamy porridge. You can pour the paste into a sealable container and refrigerate it at this stage, so you have it on hand to make up any time within the next 3–4 days.

For 4 generous bowls, measure out the paste and rice flour into a small saucepan. Blend in cold water until the mixture is the consistency of pouring cream. Add the sugar. Bring to the boil and simmer until the sugar has dissolved. The mixture should be like a dark, glossy mud pool, custard-like in consistency but still pourable. Serve hot or warm, with a spoon.

Drizzle a little coconut cream over the top of each serving or sprinkle with toasted white sesame seeds if you wish.

SERVES 4

soy milk custards with ginger syrup and spiced fruit

Fresh soy milk curd can be purchased ready-made from most Asian supermarkets.

500g fresh soy milk curd/custard
Ginger and Lemon Grass Syrup (see below)
Five Spice Roasted Pineapple and Mango (see opposite)

Use a wide gelato-style scoop to shave layers of the curd into 6 ramekins or Asian bowls. Place the dishes in a roasting pan and fill the pan with hot water to come halfway up the dishes. Cover the roasting pan with foil. Carefully transfer the pan to an oven preheated to 180°C. Heat for 15 minutes.

Serve the warm soy milk custards drizzled with 2–3 tablespoons warmed Ginger and Lemon Grass Syrup. Garnish with the syruped ginger. Place the Five Spice Roasted Pineapple and Mango on a side plate and serve extra syrup in a jug. Alternatively, you can serve the custards chilled with warm syrup.

SERVES 6

ginger and lemon grass syrup

This is great with soy milk custards, but another delicious idea is chilled melon, sliced persimmon and feijoas served in a large bowl or platter with the syrup strained over the fruit. Garnish with the syrupy ginger shreds.

5cm piece fresh ginger, peeled and julienned
1 stalk lemon grass (white part only)
½ cup sugar
1½ cups water

Place the ingredients in a small saucepan and bring to the boil. Simmer until the liquid is reduced by half and syrupy. The ginger should be almost translucent.

MAKES 1 CUP

five spice roasted pineapple and mango

Roasting the spices and fruits together brings out the best of both. I've accentuated some of the Chinese five spice flavours by adding some as whole spices. Tangy and fragrant tropical fruit flavours married with the seductive wafts of exotic spices are hard to resist. Other fruits such as feijoa, persimmon, golden queen peaches and lady-finger bananas would also work well in this recipe.

1 fresh whole pineapple, peeled and cored
2 fresh ripe mangoes, peeled
¾ cup shaved palm sugar
½ teaspoon Chinese five spice powder
zest and juice of 1 orange
4 whole star anise
1 cinnamon quill, broken into 3–4 pieces
1 teaspoon whole cloves

Preheat the oven to 200°C. Cut the fruit into largish chunks or pieces and place in an ovenproof dish. Combine the palm sugar, five spice and orange zest and sprinkle over the fruit. Pour the orange juice over and toss gently to coat. Poke the remaining spices in amongst the fruit. Roast the fruit until tinged golden brown and hot (about 15 minutes). Remove the whole spices before serving if you wish. Serve with vanilla ice cream or mascarpone or with Asian-style puddings such as almond jelly, and warmed Soy Milk Custards (see opposite).

SERVES 6

eating outdoors

Just about all food tastes better when eaten outdoors. Whether you're making the most of those long summer days or enjoying a sunny winter's day with a crisp nip in the air, here's a collection of favourite recipes to make it even more enjoyable!

THAI FISH CAKES

    CUCUMBER RELISH

SZECHWAN PEPPER ROASTED BEEF FILLET WITH CORIANDER AND CASHEW PESTO

RIBS THAT ROCK!

BOBBY'S SIMPLE ASIAN SLAW

BARBECUE OMAHA SCALLOPS WITH GINGER SHALLOT SAUCE

SEARED SCALLOP AND RICE NOODLE SALAD

CORIANDER AND BASIL NOODLE FRITTERS

BULGOLGI SESAME BEEF

BARBECUE CHICKEN WRAPPED IN KAFFIR LIME LEAVES

thai fish cakes

500g gurnard, terakihi or
  snapper
½ cup iced water
4 tablespoons red curry paste
2 tablespoons fish sauce
1 teaspoon sugar
½ teaspoon ground white
  pepper
1 egg
1 cup finely sliced green beans
  or snake beans
2 kaffir lime leaves, midrib
  removed, finely shredded
2 tablespoons coriander leaves
about 500ml oil for deep
  frying

Blend the fish in a processor at low speed, gradually adding iced water until the mixture is smooth and sticky. This will take about 15 minutes. Add the red curry paste, fish sauce, sugar and pepper and the egg and blend until the mixture thickens.

Transfer the mixture to a bowl and add the beans, kaffir lime leaves and coriander. Mix well to combine.

Heat the oil in a wok or frying pan over a medium heat. With wet hands form the fish mixture into golf-ball-sized balls, flattening them slightly into cakes. Fry in batches until golden brown, turning them over once during cooking. Serve with a sweet chilli sauce or Cucumber Relish.

SERVES 4

cucumber relish

1 telegraph cucumber or 2–3
  Lebanese cucumbers
2 shallots, chopped
2 red or orange chillies
2 cloves garlic, finely chopped
1 tablespoon sugar
4 tablespoons rice wine
  vinegar or wine vinegar
1 teaspoon salt
1 tablespoon coriander leaves
extra sliced chilli for garnish

Peel the cucumber, cut lengthwise into quarters and then slice into small pieces. Combine with the shallots in a bowl and set aside.

Use a mortar and pestle to grind together the chilli, garlic and sugar, then stir in the vinegar and salt. Heat in a small saucepan until the sugar has dissolved and the flavours have amalgamated. Cool before pouring over the cucumber and shallots. Stir through the coriander and sprinkle with the extra chilli.

MAKES ABOUT 1½ CUPS

szechwan pepper roasted beef fillet with coriander and cashew pesto

1.8–2kg whole beef eye fillet

Marinade
⅓ **cup light soy sauce**
⅓ **cup dark soy sauce**
⅓ **cup Shao Hsing wine or**
   sherry
1 teaspoon sesame oil

2–3 tablespoons vegetable oil
½ **cup Szechwan peppercorns,**
   toasted and ground finely
Coriander and Cashew Pesto
   (see page 13)

Trim the beef fillet of silver-skin. Blend the marinade ingredients together in a shallow dish and turn the beef in this to coat. Marinate for 1 hour (if time allows), turning the beef periodically to ensure the marinade penetrates the fillet evenly.

Preheat the oven to 200°C. Lift the beef from the marinade and drain. Pat dry with paper towels. Lightly oil the fillet by brushing with the vegetable oil. Heat a grill plate or large frying pan until very hot and sear the beef on all sides until golden brown. Tip the ground Szechwan pepper into an oven dish and then roll the beef in the spice, coating it evenly.

Roast in the oven until cooked to the preferred degree of doneness. As a guide: 10 minutes per 500g for rare beef, 15 minutes per 500g for medium.

Serve with the Coriander and Cashew Pesto and some homemade potato chips made with a floury potato such as Agria. A salad of watercress, coriander, Thai sweet basil, orange segments and red onion would just top it off.

ribs that rock!

I first tried these on an Asian slaw at Restaurant Bobby Chinn in Hanoi, where the ribs are marinated overnight, then steamed, cold smoked and grilled to order. The techniques used for these lip-smacking barbecue ribs incorporate the Cantonese method of steaming pork ribs which Bobby's grandmother, my mum and I still use — the meat remains tender and juicy.

The flavours here are a mix of cuisines as Bobby is Chinese-Egyptian — born in Auckland but grew up in California.

2kg piece meaty pork ribs

Spice Rub Mix

6 tablespoons brown sugar
5–6 teaspoons La Chinata
   bitter-sweet smoked paprika
3 tablespoons chopped fresh
   sage leaves
3–4 teaspoons salt

Sweet and Tangy Sauce

½ cup tart apple syrup, or
   apple cider vinegar syrup
   made by simmering 1 cup
   apple cider vinegar with
   6 tablespoons sugar until
   reduced by half
4 tablespoons tomato sauce or
   ketchup
4 tablespoons Spice Rub Mix
2 tablespoons instant coffee or
   2 shots espresso coffee

Buy the meaty pork ribs in a whole sheet or piece and get your butcher to crack them in half. Combine all the ingredients for the Spice Rub Mix and rub over the ribs, reserving 4 tablespoons for the sauce. Leave to marinate for up to an hour. Cut the sheet of ribs into 2 or 3 pieces to fit your steamer and steam for 15–20 minutes until cooked through and tender. If you don't have a steamer put the ribs on a plate on a trivet in an ordinary saucepan with 2cm of boiling water in the bottom. The steaming stops the ribs from drying out and will render any fat off if they are at all fatty.

Bobby smokes the ribs over green tea before grilling them. I use smoked paprika in the rub instead and then brown and char them over the barbecue. This works well and eliminates the smoking step, but do try it Bobby's way if you have time. Cut between the bones and pile them onto a warm platter.

Place all the ingredients for the sauce into a microwave-proof jug and microwave on high power for 2 minutes. Stir briskly. Alternatively, heat in a small saucepan until hot, stirring until the coffee has dissolved if using the instant variety. Pour into a jug to serve with the ribs. Large napkins and finger bowls are advised. This is ideal accompanied by a side dish of Bobby's Simple Asian Slaw (see page 102).

SERVES 5–6

Note: La Chinata smoked paprika and tart apple syrup are available from specialist food stores.

bobby's simple asian slaw

2 cups finely shredded red and green cabbage

1 red capsicum, thinly sliced

1 yellow capsicum, thinly sliced

2 teaspoons minced or finely grated ginger

1 cup seasoned rice wine vinegar (such as sushi vinegar)

2 tablespoons sugar

2 tablespoons sesame oil

2 tablespoons coriander leaves and 1 tablespoon toasted sesame seeds (optional)

Combine the vegetables with the ginger in a bowl. Whisk together the vinegar, sugar and sesame oil, mixing until the sugar has dissolved. Pour the dressing over the slaw, mixing in a little at a time until it is amalgamated.

If you wish, sprinkle with coriander leaves and toasted sesame seeds and toss through.

SERVES 5–6

barbecue omaha scallops with ginger shallot sauce

In the evenings, just beside the main street in Dalat in Vietnam's central highlands, shellfish are cooked to order. Whether they are cooked in their shells and anointed with a simple shallot oil dressing or plopped into steaming bowls of broth and rice noodles, the billowing steam and the midget blue and red plastic stools the customers sit on to eat and chat create an atmosphere that is always lively, festive and convivial.

I made this dish one Easter at Omaha, just north of Auckland, when a strong surf washed up a harvest of scallops along the tidemark. Placing them in a bucket of seawater for a couple of hours helped remove a lot of the sand. Fresh pipis and tuatuas are also good cooked this way.

1 dozen fresh scallops in the half shell
3 tablespoons Ginger, Shallot and Chilli Sauce (see page 12)
1 tablespoon coarsely chopped coriander, Italian flat-leafed parsley or snipped chives
ground Szechwan peppercorns
1 lime, halved crosswise

Pat the scallops dry and replace into the half shell. If they are small, place 2–3 into a scallop shell. Spoon a dab of the Ginger, Shallot and Chilli Sauce over each serving and sprinkle with the chosen herb and a pinch of pepper.

Place the shells on a hot barbecue grill along with the halved limes, cut surface down. Cook until the scallops have lost their translucency and the roe is bright coral in colour. Serve straight away with the grilled lime to squeeze over (the brief grilling heightens the flavour and makes the lime easier to juice).

SERVES 2

seared scallop and rice noodle salad

Scallops have a natural affinity with Asian flavours and limes.

2 dozen fresh scallops
1 tablespoon grated ginger
1 teaspoon sesame oil
200g dried rice stick noodles
¼ cup coriander leaves
1 tablespoon each of mint,
    Thai sweet basil and
    Vietnamese mint leaves
2 spring onions, diagonally
    sliced
1 cup mung bean sprouts,
    blanched snow peas or sugar
    snaps
1 teaspoon peanut oil
1 tablespoon toasted sesame
    seeds
extra lime wedges for serving

Dressing
1 red chilli, sliced
2 tablespoons fish sauce
juice and zest of 1 lime
2 teaspoons palm sugar or
    brown sugar

Clean the scallops if required. Pat dry with paper towels. Mix with the ginger and sesame oil and set aside.

Drop the rice noodles into a saucepan of boiling water and cook for 3 minutes. Rinse under cold water, drain and allow to cool. Place the noodles on a platter and strew with the herbs and bean sprouts or snow peas.

Combine the dressing ingredients, stirring to dissolve the sugar. Taste and adjust seasoning if necessary. Toss through the noodles.

Heat the oil in a frying pan until hot. Sear the scallops until golden and when they have just lost their translucency, remove from the pan with tongs and place on top of the salad. Sprinkle with the sesame seeds. Pass around the extra lime wedges to squeeze over the salad.

SERVES 4

coriander and basil noodle fritters

Always a hit with a crowd, these crispy, light fritters are a fabulous way of getting the outdoor party going. They can also be cooked on a barbecue hot plate if you want to be where the action is. Serve these pass-arounds on a big platter with a bowl of sweet chilli sauce to dunk them into or use them as a base for toppings.

**200g dried egg noodles
(2 nests or skeins)**
boiling water
2 large eggs
4 tablespoons plain flour
½ teaspoon baking powder
**2 tablespoons chopped
coriander**
**6–8 sweet basil leaves,
chopped**
**3 tablespoons sweet chilli
sauce**
½ teaspoon salt
**freshly ground black pepper or
Szechwan peppercorns**
**pure or light olive oil or
vegetable oil**
**extra sweet chilli sauce for
dipping**

Place the noodles in a heatproof bowl and pour boiling water over to cover. Leave to soften. Separate the noodles with a fork as they soften. Drain the noodles.

Beat the eggs in a large bowl until frothy. Sift in the flour and baking powder and whisk until smooth. Add the noodles and the remaining ingredients, except for the oil and dipping sauce. There should be only enough batter to allow the noodles to adhere together and the desired effect is lacy fritters rather than dense pikelets.

Heat the oil in a frying pan. Using a tablespoon and fork, twist the noodles into bundles and slip them into the pan. Don't coil the noodles too tightly otherwise the fritters will not be delicate and crisp. Cook until golden brown on one side and then turn over to brown the other side, pressing down lightly. Drain on paper towels. Serve on a platter with a small bowl of sweet chilli sauce for dipping into.

These are good topped with sautéed prawns or scallops combined with a little lime zest, mint and mayonnaise.

MAKES ABOUT 18–20

Don't forget napkins

for sticky fingers.

bulgolgi sesame beef

Although it takes a little forward planning to get perfect results with the beef, the cooking is over within seconds as the thinly sliced meat is quickly seared. Have the hot rice, a platter of lettuce, fruit, kimchi and the dipping sauce ready before you cook the meat.

450g beef fillet
1 tablespoon toasted sesame
  seeds
4 spring onions,
  coarsely chopped
3 cloves garlic, finely chopped
1 tablespoon grated ginger
1 tablespoon dark soy sauce
1 tablespoon rice wine
2 tablespoons water
1 teaspoon brown sugar
1 tablespoon sesame oil
freshly ground black pepper
2 tablespoons vegetable oil
extra toasted sesame seeds

Wrap the fillet of beef in plastic food wrap and put into the freezer for about an hour. This will semi-freeze the beef and make it easier to slice thinly.

Meanwhile, make the marinade: crush the sesame seeds using a mortar and pestle and put into a bowl with the rest of the ingredients except the vegetable oil and extra sesame seeds.

Cut the meat across the grain into very thin discs and put into the marinade for at least 1 hour. When you are ready to cook, oil a heavy cast-iron frying pan or char-grilling pan and heat until smoking. Put the meat on it in a single layer and cook very quickly on both sides. You can also use a barbecue hot plate. Serve hot off the grill.

Arrange on a platter a pile of iceberg or cos lettuce leaves, some sliced crisp apple, nashi pear or persimmons, shredded spring onion (soaked in iced water until it curls), kimchi (Korean pickled cabbage, which has chilli, garlic, ginger and spring onion and is readily available in Asian supermarkets) and a bowl of Dipping Sauce (see below). To eat, place some Bulgolgi on a lettuce leaf, add some of each of the other accompaniments from the platter and roll up into a bundle. Dip into the sauce and eat with hot rice.

SERVES 4–5

Dipping Sauce
1 tablespoon soybean paste
  or miso
1 teaspoon crushed garlic
2 teaspoons Korean red
  pepper sauce
1 teaspoon vegetable oil
2 tablespoons water

Place all the ingredients in a small saucepan and simmer gently for 5 minutes to amalgamate the flavours. Pour into a bowl for dipping.

barbecue chicken wrapped in kaffir lime leaves

Marinade
1 tablespoon runny honey
1 tablespoon vegetable oil
½ teaspoon five spice powder
1 tablespoon hoisin sauce
2 tablespoons light soy sauce
½ cup Chinese rice wine
2 cloves garlic, finely chopped
1 tablespoon grated ginger

6 chicken thighs, skinned and
   cut into 5cm cubes
large kaffir lime leaves
bamboo satay sticks, soaked in
   cold water for ½ hour

Combine the marinade ingredients in a large bowl, add the chicken and mix to coat well, then leave to marinate for at least 2 hours.

Take each piece of chicken and wrap it in a lime leaf before threading onto a satay stick. If the leaves are too small, use 2 to cover the piece of chicken. Put 4 pieces of chicken onto each satay stick. Cook on the hot barbecue for about 8 minutes, turning often. Eat hot off the barbecue with salad or with fragrant Thai rice and Cucumber Relish (see page 98).

SERVES 6 AS A STARTER

glossary

Bean thread vermicelli is made from mung beans and is gluten free. It needs soaking in warm water before using in stir-fries, salads or spring rolls and it picks up the flavour of sauces and seasonings.

Chilli bean sauce is a hot, pungent bean sauce that goes particularly well with noodles.

Chilli oil is made by infusing crushed dried chillies in oil. Use it to add heat to dishes or as a dipping condiment.

Chillies come in many varieties and colours. Generally the smaller they are, such as Thai bird's eye chillies, the hotter they are.

Choy sum or flowering Chinese cabbage are characterised by bright green stems and edible yellow flowers.

Daikon radish or Chinese turnip is a giant-sized white root vegetable with a mustardy bite.

Fermented bean curd is made from soybean curd and is packed in brine. It is referred to as Asia's answer to blue cheese. Rich in flavour and aroma, it also comes with added chilli.

Fish sauce is used in Thai, Vietnamese, Lao and Cambodian cuisines in place of soy sauce. It has a distinct salted fish flavour.

Five spice powder combines the flavours of ground cinnamon, star anise, cloves, Szechwan pepper and fennel.

Ground brown bean sauce is made from mashed fermenting salted soybeans. It is spicy and aromatic and lighter in colour than black bean sauce.

Hoisin sauce is a rich, robust red/brown combination of fermented soybeans, plums, garlic, sugar, salt and spices.

Kaffir lime leaves have a vibrant fresh lime scent. They are either used whole to flavour curries and stocks or the midrib is removed and the leaf finely shredded to be added into salads, marinades and dressings. The fruit has a knobbly peel which is used in curry pastes.

Lemon grass is a tall, pale-green-stemmed herb with a distinct lemony aroma and flavour. Generally the thick base of the stem is used in cooking as the leaves are fibrous.

Lup cheong (Chinese sausages) The literal translation is 'waxed sausages', which describes their waxy appearance, rather than anything to do with their making. Made from pork, pork fat, salt, sugar and traditionally flavoured with rose-scented rice wine and air-dried. The supermarket product is usually found vacuum-packed.

Mirin is a straw-coloured, sweet-cooking condiment, made from rice and distilled alcohol. Use it in place of vinegar in dressings for a milder flavour.

Palm sugar is sold in round cakes or cylinders. Its distinctive caramel flavour lends itself to savoury and sweet cookery. As it is relatively soft, it can be shaved off with a sharp knife or coarsely grated. It melts readily when heated.

Seven spice powder is a popular Japanese seasoning for table use or for sprinkling over meats before roasting or barbecuing. Typically a mix of hot chilli pepper, sancho pepper, toasted sesame seeds, poppy seeds, green nori flakes, dried, flaked tangerine peel and flax seeds.

Soy sauces Use light soy for dipping and marinades and dark soy to give a rich colour in braised or slow-cooked dishes.

Szechwan peppercorns are actually small, dried pinkish-brown berries with more fragrance than ordinary pepper and a delayed but mild heat.

Tamarind is used to impart a sweet tang to marinades, sauces and dressings.

Thai sweet basil has a spicy, aniseed and mild licorice taste. The deep green, tear-drop shaped leaves are attached at nodules all the way up the purplish stems.

Tofu or bean curd is a pressed curd made from soy bean milk. Firm and soft (silken) tofu is available in blocks in the chiller cabinet of most Asian supermarkets. The soft variety is best in soups and sauces, whereas the firm tofu is more suitable for stir-fries, braises or deep-frying.

Vietnamese mint, laksa leaf or hot mint is not a true mint despite the name. The spicy, elongated, deep green leaves have a delayed heat. It is used in laksa curry soup, curry pastes and used raw in Vietnamese and Thai-style salads.

For a more comprehensive guide, refer to *Discovering Asian Ingredients*, a practical guide to sourcing, choosing and using Asian ingredients.

index